BRITISH WADERS
IN THEIR HAUNTS

BRITISH WADERS IN THEIR HAUNTS

by

S. BAYLISS SMITH

M.A., M.B.O.U.

*Illustrated with fifty-three photographs by the author
and twenty-six by other bird photographers,
with three plates of Waders in flight by*

BASIL LAKER

LONDON   G. BELL & SONS, LTD   1950

To
Jeremy and Timothy
and other bird
watchers of the future

First published, 1950

Printed in Great Britain by
Billing and Sons Ltd., Guildford and Esher
G35

Foreword

AT a time when books on British Birds appear with the regularity and abundance of mushrooms on a well-composted bed, a word of explanation is required to justify the appearance of yet another book on the subject. The explanation is really contained in the title of the book. Most birds in Britain have had their portraits taken again and again with a skill which may well be the despair of anyone who is taking up this exacting hobby for the first time. But the waders—at least the migrant waders—are an exception. The transitory nature of their visits here, coupled with the inaccessibility of their haunts on mud-flats and saltings, puts them in a class apart. Nine out of ten photographs of birds are normally taken at the nest. Unless one is prepared to undertake an Arctic expedition and spend a season in Greenland, Spitzbergen or the Taimyr Peninsula, this possibility is ruled out with the majority of our northern-nesting waders. To photograph them at all in this country one must explore what opportunities there are in and around the great estuaries which they frequent. Fortunately for one who would seek to portray them, there is one recurring factor in a shore-wader's life which cannot be gainsaid—the rising tide. When their feeding grounds out on the tidal ooze are flooded, they have no option but to seek temporary sanctuary elsewhere. Some slip off inland, but a great many resort to mud banks or shingles, or to islands which are out of the reach of the tide. It is there that they may be interviewed if due precautions are taken, and in the following pages I have tried to convey some of the intense pleasure that is to be found in this exhilarating pursuit.

I owe my initiation into the craft of 'wait and see' photography to Guy B. Farrar, whose book *The Feathered Folk of an Estuary* was an early source of inspiration to me. His subsequent kindness and hospitality on my visits to the Cheshire Dee have been greatly appreciated. In the preparation of this book I should like to acknowledge with gratitude the help of another wader enthusiast, Grahame des Forges, whose library has been placed at my disposal, and whose company I have had on several memorable expeditions. He has also allowed me to reproduce three of his own photographs, and through his kindness I have been able to contact three Dutch photographers whose portraits of species seldom encountered in this country are a very welcome addition to this book. J. E. Sluiters, F. P. J. Kooymans and J. V. Vijverberg are all bird watchers who have discovered the fascination of wader photography on the lagoons and mud-flats of their native Holland, and I am deeply indebted to them for permission to reproduce some of their charming wader portraits here. I should also like to thank Ralph Chislett, G. K. Yeates, Arnold H. Smith, Stanton Whitaker, T. M. Fowler and R. H. Hallam for contributing photographs of species that I have not yet had the good fortune to encounter. In the preparation of distribution maps of the resident species I am very grateful for permission to incorporate material compiled by W. B. Alexander and James Fisher. In my quest for new hunting-grounds on the South Coast I should like to pay tribute to the great assistance that John Reynolds has given me, and it is in a large measure due to him that I have met with success on this rather difficult stretch of coast. Mention will be made later in this book of Basil Laker, the young artist whose plates of waders in flight are included, but I should like to add his name to the list of those to whom my sincere thanks are due. In matters relating to typing and in the checking of proofs, G. P. Burstow has been a very valuable friend and ally, and, lastly, I should like to record my gratitude to one, who, though she has good reason to describe herself as ' a bird watcher's widow,' has shown remarkable understanding and forbearance, and has herself caught sufficient of the enthusiasm of this hobby to accompany me for long vigils on hard rocks and in stuffy hides, to gain a closer acquaintance of those feathered wanderers that flock to an island sanctuary when the tide is high.

The Junior School,   S. BAYLISS SMITH
Brighton College
June, 1949

Acknowledgments

Kind permission has been granted by the following to include copyright material: H. J. Massingham for extracts from *Birds of the Seashore* on pp. 79, 87-8, 107-8; Edward Arnold and Co. for permission to include passages from *A Summer on the Yenesei*, by M. D. Haviland, on pp. 92-3, 104; John Murray for a passage from *Siberia in Europe*, by H. Seebohm, on p. 60, and *The Ibis* for a passage from an article by H. L. Popham (1897, p. 105) on p. 60.

For historical data on the work of early ornithologists the author begs to acknowledge his debt to material contained in E. M. Nicholson's *Birds in England*.

Contents

List of Illustrations

Photographs are by the author except where otherwise stated

I

The Unfolding of Wader Mysteries

THE first book on British birds, William Turner's *Avium Præcipuarum*, an essay on ornithology that was a mere minor incident in the literary output of an eccentric physician and divine in the reign of Henry the Eighth, contains but few allusions to the family of waders. A century later we find another physician, Sir Thomas Browne, making shrewd comments on the birds of his native Norfolk, but the desultory scraps of notes and the handful of his letters on ornithology that have been preserved serve only as a reminder of what might have been, had the author of the *Religio Medici* written a full-length treatise on the birds of a county which is still one of the most favoured in all England for the variety of its bird-life.

Almost a contemporary of Browne was Francis Willughby, a Warwickshire gentleman, who, with John Ray, the greatest naturalist of his age, made the first serious attempt at a systematic study of our native birds. *The Ornithology*, by Willughby, published under Ray's editorship four years after the author's decease in 1672, is our first Handbook on British Birds. As a pioneer work it opened the way for succeeding generations, but it required another century of systematic field-work before the study of birds emerged from the realm of anecdote, legend and folk-lore.

George Montagu and Gilbert White, each in his own particular way, were the real founders of field ornithology and the love of birds in England. Of the two, Montagu made more, if not greater, discoveries, and his travels took him over the length and breadth of the country. But because his observations were put down in a form which had nothing to recommend it to posterity, his name is practically forgotten. Gilbert White, the parson of Selborne, who rarely stirred beyond the boundaries of his parish, is known and loved as few other writers on Natural History have ever been, and he is still read today, not on account of his discoveries, but because of the whimsical charm which pervades all that he wrote. White was content with composing short monographs on his favourite species: Montagu produced a monumental *Ornithological Dictionary* which he presented to the public in 1802, and twelve years later appended an admirable *Supplement*. It was perhaps unfortunate that it was not Montagu's book but Thomas Bewick's *History of British Birds* (Vol. 1, 1797; Vol. 2, 1804) which became the standard work for ornithologists in this country during the next generation. The exquisite woodcuts with which he illustrated his books revealed him as a superb craftsman, and his mordant illustrative humour appealed to the contemporary world in a way that made his book a ' best-seller ' for the next thirty years.

If we turn over the pages of Bewick today, we cannot help but be deeply impressed by the detailed knowledge of the resident and migratory birds of the English countryside which had been accumulated in his day; but when we come to the section on waders we enter an unfamiliar world—a world peopled by birds that have an almost mediæval aura of mystery surrounding them. We encounter Godwits described as Red, Cinereous, Lesser and Cambridge; we find two species of Turnstone and a remarkable bird called the Gambet; we discover another wader called the Purre which we think must be a Dunlin until we find a Dunlin described separately on another page; we read of Sandpipers, Red-legged, Ash-coloured, Brown, Greenwich and Aberdeen. It is all most confusing, and it seems fairly obvious that many of the names have been invented on the spot by fowlers who were at a loss to account for the curiously plumaged wanderers that had fallen to their guns, or been trapped in their nets, in various parts of the country. And most of the species are thought to be resident, though no one ever seems to have found their eggs.

After a little reflection the realisation dawns on us that this confusion can have only this explanation. Three salient factors which characterise the wader tribes have as yet been scarcely recognised: First, that most adult waders undergo a metamorphosis of plumage with the approach of the breeding-season that entirely alters their appearance; secondly, that young birds in their first plumage often look quite different from their parents; and thirdly, that the majority of these birds nest in regions so far north that another century of research and Polar exploration was required to track them to their haunts.

From the constantly recurring references to waders as table-birds in the pages of Bewick, it is apparent that the main interest in them was still gastronomic. "Much esteemed by epicures . . . sells very high . . . delicate and excellent food . . . a delicious and well-flavoured dish . . . sought after with great eagerness." Almost every species is described with an emphasis on its desirability as an item on the menu. This is understandable when we realise that one of the main problems of our forefathers was to procure fresh meat for the winter months. The dove-cote and the ice-house were a partial remedy, but it was the marshman who could provide the delicacies. Hence the waggon-

Redshanks line the water's edge at an island roost

Oyster-Catchers arriving as the tide covers the estuary

Congestion at high tide. A Knot and two Dunlins in the foreground: Redshanks mass behind them

Turnstones, Sanderlings, Dunlins and a lone Redshank share a sandstone hummock

loads of Godwits that plied between Peterborough and London, and the trade in hand-fattened Ruffs that brought Lincolnshire a considerable reputation until the draining of the fens and the extinction of our breeding-stock through excessive netting on their 'tilting-grounds' brought a profitable trade to its close. Its continuance was rendered unnecessary through economic factors. There is a more satisfying meat-supply in a ship-load of imported beef or mutton than in a few waggon-loads of shore-birds. The days of mass slaughter were drawing to a close, and, as so often happens, the means of livelihood of a few hardy folk—and the fen men were the hardiest of our race—became the sport of the few. Punt-gunning became a fashionable occupation for sportsmen-ornithologists. Their record 'bags' make impressive but nauseating reading. As an instance may be quoted E. T. Booth's account of a 'successful' day on Breydon: " I remember one autumn, that, besides above thirty Knots, I obtained at a single discharge of the punt gun, specimens in larger or smaller numbers of the following species: Ruff, Redshank, Pigmy-Curlew, Dunlin, Stint, Greenshank, Spotted Redshank and Golden Plover." Or again: " Seventy Knots and twenty-four Godwits, the whole being the result of a single shot, were picked up, at least half as many more being swept away by the flowing tide before those nearest at hand could be gathered up. "

It is to be feared that this indiscriminate slaughter is not yet a thing of the past, and sackfuls of Knots and Dunlins still arrive mysteriously at London hotels, where they are boiled down into soups, or served up in some expensive disguise.

4

August: Turnstones still in breeding-plumage and partial moult

But it is a sign of a changing attitude to bird-life in this country that often enough on a visit to the mud flats one comes across a fellow enthusiast who, armed with nothing more lethal than a pair of binoculars or a telescope, is content to watch and to record, and possibly (for I have known it done) to put to flight a flock of birds whose lives were in jeopardy because of the stealthy approach of a man with a gun.

The state of confusion about our waders that prevailed in Bewick's day was not allowed to continue much longer. The standard of observation which Montagu and White had set was not forgotten, and a new school of ornithologists appeared who rapidly sorted out the complexities of plumage presented by the seasonal change in wader species. By the time William Yarrell came to publish his *British Birds* (1837-1843) all the main difficulties had been overcome, but there still remained the mystery of their breeding-haunts.

In the year that saw the completion of Yarrell's work, a German ornithologist, Dr. von Middendorff, penetrated into the little-known Taimyr Peninsula in Asiatic Siberia. On the limitless tundra fronting the Arctic Sea, in a desolate land far beyond the limit of forest growth, he was rewarded with the discovery of breeding-haunts of Grey Plover, Little Stint, Temminck's Stint and Grey Phalarope. His discoveries excited the imagination of ornithologists in this country—and the hunt was on. A few years later an Englishman, John Wolley, determined to explore the possibilities of northern Sweden and what is now Finland as a breeding-haunt of some hitherto undiscovered species. In the great marsh of Muonioniska, on June 17th, 1853, he first heard the Jack Snipe's courting-song, and soon afterwards he succeeded in finding its nest, so clearing up another mystery. To his credit also goes the discovery of the breeding-grounds of Bar-Tailed Godwit and Spotted Redshank in those northern regions, and he may justly claim to have done real pioneer work in this field.

5

Sanderlings and Dunlins move nearer the hide

Another ten years passed before any further wader mysteries were solved, and then, curiously enough, it was not an arctic-nesting species that yielded up its secrets, but a bird that breeds as far south as the former Baltic States. Though German ornithologists had been aware of the facts for some years, it was not until 1863 that Prof. Newton made known to incredulous British naturalists that the Green Sandpiper habitually laid its eggs in the old nest of a Missel Thrush or of some other tree-nesting species. It was an aberration of nesting behaviour that shook the conservative ornithologists of the day. What next would these waders be doing?

There still remained a few species to be tracked down, and the subsequent discoveries of breeding-haunts of Knot and Sanderling serve as a reminder that the unfolding of wader mysteries is closely linked with the history of Polar exploration. Macfarlane found the first authenticated Sanderling eggs in the arctic solitudes of Franklin Bay, and the Nares Polar Expedition found them breeding in Grinnell Land in 1876. Dr. Bessels of the *Polaris* captured nestlings on the west side of Greenland, but it was not until 1908 that the first American nest was found.

No history of wader discoveries is complete without mention of Seebohm and Harvie-Brown, who penetrated to the mouth of the Petchora River in European Siberia in 1875. It was their ambition to record for Europe certain wader species whose haunts were undiscovered or whose nests had only been found until then in Asiatic Siberia. The Grey Plover, the Little Stint and the

6

Curlew-Sandpiper were the main object of their search. They succeeded brilliantly with the first two species, but had to admit defeat with the third, and it was left to H. L. Popham to be the first to run to earth the elusive Curlew-Sandpiper. Near the mouth of the River Yenisei in Asiatic Siberia he found the first nest of this species in 1897, though Alaskan eggs had previously been found in 1883.

The Knot was one of the last of the waders to yield to the searchers. Though Sabine had reported the bird to be nesting on Melville Island as early as 1820, nothing further was known of it until Colonel Fielden and Chichester Hart, naturalists on board H.M.S. *Alert* and H.M.S. *Discovery* of the Nares Expedition, found nestlings in Grinnell Land in 1876. It was not until the turn of the century that the first eggs were found—by Dr. Walter on the Taimyr Peninsula. The American species of Knot, a ruddier bird in summer plumage than ours, eluded the searchers until an even later date. Admiral Peary's expedition eventually discovered it, again in Grinnell Land, and the Admiral himself had the pleasure of photographing it on the nest in 1909.

Does this bring us to the end of the quest? Very nearly—but not quite. There still remain two species on the British list whose breeding-haunts have yet to be discovered, but both are birds of such exceeding rarity in their occurrence in these islands that there would be no point in mentioning them were it not for the intriguing fact that no one has yet discovered their nests. The Siberian Pectoral Sandpiper and the Grey-Rumped Sandpiper, both birds of Asiatic Siberia that have strayed out of their normal range and into our records, have yet to have their nests and eggs described, but it will have to be left to a Russian naturalist to do so, for these birds are well out of the range of an Englishman's ornithological travels.

Now that the mystery of their breeding-grounds has been almost un-ravelled, the emphasis in the study of waders has shifted. The problems that now await solution are quite as complex and difficult as those that faced the older generation of ornithologists. They concern the relation of the various wader tribes to one another—for no family of birds has caused more trouble to the systematist than the *Charadriiformes*, and geographical variations of size and plumage are still a matter for contention between those who seek to differentiate sub-species within the various wader families. They concern, too, the world-wide wanderings of these nomadic creatures whose vast migratory flights are a source of perpetual wonder to those who care to study them. We know, for example, that the Sanderling, a bird that breeds so far within the Arctic Circle that a Polar expedition is required to track it to its haunts, is found outside the breeding-season not only on the coast of Britain but on the beaches of Africa and India, of Borneo, Hawaii and Australia. When the brief arctic summer is over—eight weeks in which to complete the whole breeding-cycle—the southward passage starts. In late July, Sanderlings are back again in our estuaries. Some stay and winter here, but the majority pass onwards ever south, ranging the shores of the world until, as the year swings through its course, that mysterious influence within their delicate organisms which dictates the direction of their travels urges them northwards at the appointed season, and once again, obeying the summons of the northlands, they span the globe and hasten to their breeding-grounds, and there, in a desolation indescribable, the ceremonies of courtship are observed, the eggs are laid, the young ones reared, whilst the unsinking sun circles the heavens, and chilling blasts from the Polar cap, a few hundred miles to the northward, come as a perpetual reminder that time is short and very precious.

To check the movements and migrations of these northing waders we have at present to limit our observations to what we see of them in their wanderings up and down the world, but an ever-growing corpus of published records of their occurrences in different countries is providing material for a scientific study of their peregrinations. Accurate records of species observed, of the times of their occurrence, of their approximate strength, and of the prevailing conditions of wind and weather, can all help in piecing together a story that is as fascinating as it is elusive. As an instance of the value of isolated observations may be cited the records that have been coming to light in recent years of waders seen resting on the sea. At one time it was thought that their vast migrations over the oceans of the world were undertaken without a break. Quite possibly the birds seen resting in this way were not following the usual custom of their kindred, but at least it must be comforting to a wader to know that it can alight on the sea if the occasion demands it. The modern method of checking the dispersal and migration of birds is by putting aluminium rings on the legs of nestlings, and, with resident species, though only about two in every hundred rings are ever recovered, the results more than justify the trouble involved. With resident waders, notably Woodcock, Snipe, Lapwing, Redshank and Curlew, most satisfactory results have been forthcoming, and every year sees an increase in our knowledge of the dispersal and migration of these birds. But how can we apply this method to the arctic-nesting species? Much as we should like a ringing expedition to Grinnell Land or the Taimyr Peninsula, the thing is just impossible, and in any case Arctic explorers have more pressing demands on their time. An occasional migrating wader may be netted and a ring attached to it, but the method does not hold out very great possibilities, though in this connection it is worth

8

A Bar-Tailed Godwit takes its stand amongst the Oyster-Catchers

An adult and three immature Redshanks in the shallows

Oyster-Catchers, Lesser and Great Black-Backed Gulls lean against the flowing tide

mentioning that a Turnstone, ringed in Co. Antrim, was later recovered in N.W. Greenland. As an occurrence it was little short of miraculous, especially in view of the fact that, until then, it was only the second Turnstone ever to have been ringed in Great Britain.

As well as sifting the evidence on migration, another trend in ornithology has been growing in the present century. Prior to recent times, with very few exceptions, the interest of ornithologists was centred on eggs and skins. A bird was not really prized until its body, stuffed with cotton-wool and supported on wires, was safely behind glass in a collector's private museum.

Today the emphasis is on the living bird. Ornithology has emerged from the museum into the open air, and it is the living bird in its behaviour and its relation to environment which is the object of study today. And the waders, possibly more than any other family of birds, show infinite variations of behaviour in the ceremonials that attend their courtship; in the individual and corporate manœuvres that they perform in the air, both in and out of the breeding-season; in 'injury-feigning' at the nest; in aggressive display when their territories are invaded; and even in the diversity of ways in which they obtain their food. Edmund Selous, J. S. Huxley, F. A. Montague, and others after them, have not been slow to realise what possibilities there are for observation and interpretation, with Ruffs on their 'tilting-grounds,' with Redshanks performing the rituals of courtship, with Oyster-Catchers indulging in their 'piping ceremonies,' and with many other waders following the pattern of behaviour which is inherent in its own species, and which is, as such, unique.

On green-marsh and salting, on mud-flat and tidal creek, may be found, at one and the same time, a zoologist's observatory, an artist's studio and a bird-watcher's paradise. But whatever purpose takes you there, beware lest you are ensnared by the charm of the wading fraternity; for once you have fallen under their spell there is no escape: their image will always be with you.

2

The Technique of Estuary Photography

EVERY year, with unfailing regularity, from mid-July and onwards into August and September, the migrant waders from the northlands invade our shores. Here in Britain our summer holiday season is at its height, but in the sub-polar regions the arctic twilight is already deepening. When the first flurries of snow come scudding across the limitless expanse of dwarf willow and reindeer moss where they have reared their young they receive the southward summons. Then, on a favourable day, the estuaries on our coasts, which for weeks past have been strangely devoid of birds, suddenly awaken to full and teeming life again. Arriving overnight in their thousands, they spread over the grey waste of mud, dibbling away in their endless quest for food—a multitude that no man can number.

This is the season of great opportunity for the tide-line photographer. Not only are the birds passing through in great strength, but the flocks contain a large proportion of young birds that have not yet learnt the fear of man; innocent waderlings whose trustfulness gives confidence to the more wary adults. At this season one can approach them openly on the mud flats, and often enough it is possible to get sufficiently near to be tempted to try for distant photographs of them there. But it is a profitless occupation. It is far better to go armed with binoculars alone. In a favourable estuary, when the tide is out, one can wander at will for an hour or two and study the plumage variations of a dozen different species. But they are always just too far away to yield satisfactory photographs. I have a score of negatives obtained in this way, but not one of them can produce a really good print. A line of minute, pearly dots by the water's edge I know to be a score of Sanderlings. I doubt if anyone else would recognise them as such. A long-billed wader, slightly blurred and very distant, I proudly claim to be a Bar-Tailed Godwit. A flurry of black-and-white birds departing in haste from a sand bar might, to an imaginative ornithologist, be a flock of Avocets or Stilts. They were, in fact, Oyster-Catchers. At the time they were all satisfying records of highly successful stalks, but as bird photographs they are, on mature reflection, entirely worthless. It is better to admit that the pictures obtained from this

Driven from their breeding-grounds, the estuary birds mass on an island sanctuary

type of stalking, though full of happy memories, are, as wader portraits, not a success. Sooner or later one is forced to the conclusion that the only way of getting to grips with these elusive creatures is to use a hide. One must don that cloak of invisibility essential for all intimate work with birds. But where is the hide to be built? Out on the mud flats the chances of success are remote. Birds working over the ooze may possibly come within range, but more likely they will not. A more promising site is where, as not infrequently happens, a tongue of land projects out into the flats. The chances of success in such a situation are greatly increased if the hide is left up as a permanent structure. I know of a hide which has been left up in just such a site for several winters, and the waders in that particular estuary have come to regard it as an essential part of the landscape, so that birds as wary as Curlews and Godwits now feed unconcernedly within a few yards of it.

But photography from a hide of this kind requires residence near the scene of operations. Grateful though I am for an opportunity of spending a few hours in a hide of this kind, the geographical limitations imposed upon me by living thirty miles away from my nearest good wader haunt cause me to regard it as not the most satisfactory method of interviewing waders. For me, the solution of the problem lies in one constant and recurring factor in a shore wader's daily life—the rising tide. Twice in every twenty-four hours the feeding grounds are flooded. Driven from their muddy haunts, they have no alternative but to seek a high-tide sanctuary. Some of them flock inland, Curlews almost invariably so, but the great majority congregate on bars and reefs that will not be flooded, or on the fringes of the estuary where they will not be disturbed, and where they may doze away the high-tide hours. A knowledge of local geography and of the habits of local birds will soon reveal the places that they mostly favour, and it is there that one can secrete oneself in their midst. The trouble with such places is that there are usually several alternative sites to which they can resort if they find that a suspicious-looking tent has suddenly appeared on their favourite resting-place.

There is no doubt that the most promising place of all is an island out in the estuary itself. It need only be a high mud bank, a shingle spit, or a reef of rocks that alone will not be covered when the rest of the estuary is flooded. An island roost of this kind has a tremendously strong attraction for all the birds that frequent the muddy wastes at low tide. Ideally it should have an area of several hundred square yards at low tide, but it should shrink to a fraction of this size at high water. If it becomes too small and the congestion of birds becomes excessive it will fail in its purpose, for the birds will leave and go elsewhere. I well remember one occasion when the tide lifted a couple of feet higher than I had anticipated, and my island was reduced to the size of a billiard table. All the waders departed and I was left for an apprehensive quarter of an hour with three Cormorants as my sole companions, the nearest of them so close that I could have touched him with a walking stick.

The height of the tide and the consequent area of an island at high water are subject to variations that have a variety of causes. Every fortnight the tides build up to a peak which coincides with a full moon or with the period midway between full moons. In the spring and autumn the equinoctial tides reach unprecedented heights, and the estuary photographer should know his island uncommonly well if he is prepared to risk these tides, for a situation of real danger may well arise. A high barometer and an off-shore wind may lower the anticipated height of the tide by a foot or more, but a low or rapidly falling barometer with an on-shore wind will have the reverse effect. Only once have I had the full force of a wave break over my hide, but the ease

A lively group of Redshanks and three Knots

with which it ripped the canvas from the uprights and drenched me to the skin left me with a very healthy respect for tidal water.

But in spite of its hazards—or more probably because of them—I look upon tidal photography as a form of adventure supremely satisfying for one who is compelled to spend his days in an orthodox and over-respectable profession. When, at six o'clock in the morning, I don my heavy woollens, climb into my rubber thigh boots and stagger off to the station with my photographic kit to catch the only train of the day that will convey me within reach of the island in time for the midday tide, I feel an expectancy and an exhilaration which have a quality all their own. The photographic results, when any are obtained, give me far more satisfaction than portraits of birds taken at their nests. These, my wader visitants, are wild and free as the wind that whistles over the estuary. There is no invisible thread of parental anxiety that draws them within range of my camera. If, under the persuasion of the rising tide, they consent to share with me the intimacy of island life for the high-tide hours, it is a compliment that fills me with a sense of privilege such as no other form of bird-watching can give. I do not wish to detract from the pleasures of nest photography. I have spent some of the happiest hours of my life interviewing birds at the nest, and I still experience a feeling of exquisite pleasure when I see, from a few feet away, a parent bird return to feed its young. But the pleasure of such an occasion cannot, in my experience, compare with the intense exhilaration that one feels when surrounded by a host of shy waders massed on a shrinking island, with every oncoming wave bringing them nearer and nearer until they are so close that it almost seems as if they will overrun the hide itself. Forgotten is the long journey; forgotten the physical strain of carrying heavy apparatus over shingle banks and mud flats, and the long wait in cramped quarters before the birds begin to arrive. The present is all that matters, and the intense excitement of trying to record in photographic form the astonishing scene before one's eyes.

It is difficult to find adequate reasons to account for the intensely moving effect that such an experience has upon one. There are many contributory causes, not least being a deep conviction that waders, like pearls, are only seen to their best advantage when threaded closely together and displayed in a beautiful setting. Or, to change the simile, one could compare a lone wader on a mud flat to a solitary soldier on Salisbury Plain, appropriate to his surroundings but hardly impressive as a spectacle. But see them both in company with a thousand others of their kind, carrying out orderly and intricate exercises, and their whole character is transformed. To be engulfed in waders for the high-tide hour is, for me, an experience that has no parallel elsewhere in the life of a naturalist. The surprising thing is that so few have discovered that such an experience is possible.

One of the first questions to be considered by the estuary photographer is the type of hide that should be employed for this kind of work. Most bird photographers evolve their own species of hide to which they become strongly attached, and they tend to regard their own pet creations as indispensable. The truth of the matter is that if certain elementary principles are followed in hide construction there is little to choose between one hide and another. Personally, for this type of photography I prefer a fairly small hide. The whole secret of success in the estuary lies in the one word 'rigidity.' I have four wooden uprights which slope inwards and bolt securely to cross-pieces at the top. When assembled, the framework stands securely on its four legs without the need of further support from guy ropes. Nor is it necessary to sink the legs into the ground, a procedure that would be quite impossible when the island is a bare outcrop of rock. A tightly fitting double layer of sacking is pulled over the framework and secured at its base with loose stones or shingle. Sacking has many advantages. It is neutral in tone, and its rough texture helps to avoid any suggestion of shine such as more closely woven fabrics are liable to give. It has the additional advantage of being easily obtained or replaced. I always carry a needle and strong thread for running repairs on the spot.

I believe that in estuary work one's chances of success are very greatly increased by using a hide of unobtrusive design and of neutral tones. I know

In the early autumn the size, shape and colour of a hide do not matter as much as later in the year. This hide was one kindly lent to me by Guy Farrar. From it he has taken many of his best photographs, and on the day I used it the birds massed round most satisfactorily, as can be seen from this photograph taken by my wife, who was in my small 'sitting' hide thirty yards away

there are many bird photographers who maintain that the colour of a hide and its shape make no difference at all. That this idea should have gained general currency is quite understandable when one considers that the experience of the majority of workers is limited to photographing birds that are possessed by a burning anxiety to return to eggs which are in danger of getting chilled, or to young ones that must be fed or perish. Under such circumstances, with the parental urge strong upon them, most birds will show a quite extraordinary disregard for danger, and they will tolerate the intrusion into their nesting haunts of hides that make no pretence whatever of matching their surroundings. But out in the estuary the conditions are quite different. The use of a high-tide roost is, for the birds that frequent the mud flats, a matter of convenience and not of necessity. If they take exception to the appearance of a hide and shy away there is no incentive whatever to make them return. They will simply use another resting place a mile away. It matters not a whit to them that you have toiled across to the island for the express purpose of interviewing them. The freedom of the estuary is theirs, and they are not particularly concerned as to which of several alternative sites they use.

Undoubtedly there are occasions when perfectly good results could be obtained from a bell-tent or even a moderate-sized marquee. In August and September when the flocks are largely composed of innocent young birds for whom the works of man have no sinister significance the size and colour of the hide do not matter a great deal. But later in the year, after the local shore-gunners have been at work, and especially during the return migration in spring and early summer, these details matter a great deal. As my visits to the estuary are confined to occasional days and week-ends, I prefer to take no chances.

The greatest enemy of the estuary photographer is without any doubt at all—wind. There are very few days in the year when there is not a fairly brisk breeze blowing, and wind can be a most insidious foe. Even though the sacking has been stretched as tightly as possible over the framework, there is generally a tendency for rippling movements to agitate the surface of one or more sides of the hide. Any such movements may well prove disastrous, and many an expedition has proved fruitless for this cause alone. It is essential to have a liberal supply of safety-pins always at hand for taking in any loose folds of material inside the hide once you are installed there. It is better to do this from inside the hide because the metallic glitter of a pin on the outside might well be a source of alarm. The larger the safety-pins, the better they serve their purpose, and here I suspect that the family man has an unfair advantage over his bachelor friends, for the type of pin known in family circles as the 'nappy' pin is wholly admirable for the purpose, and, in my own household, as my long-suffering wife will testify, the nursery has been discovered to be a most fruitful source of supply.

And now what of the photographic apparatus suitable for this type of work? First and foremost I would stress the necessity of a reflex camera. Accurate and instantaneous focusing of birds that are constantly on the move is an absolute essential. With the ordinary plate camera, the instrument most favoured by nest photographers, the difficulties are considerable. One could, of course, focus beforehand on a suitable shelf of rock or ridge of shingle

Redshanks crowd together on the sea-washed rocks. Dunlins and Sanderlings seek
a dryer station

and hope that the birds will occupy that particular spot, but the limitations of this technique are immediately apparent to anyone who has tried his hand at this kind of work. With a reflex camera one can follow the birds wherever they go. Often enough an attractive grouping is glimpsed or a rare newcomer identified for the first time on the focusing screen as one ' pans ' the camera cautiously backwards and forwards over the assembled birds. In any case the pleasure of seeing the whole scene in Nature's own colours on the focusing screen is one that I personally would not forego whatever advances may be made in camera technique.

A long focus lens is an absolute necessity. The occasions when one can get a satisfactory image with a lens of less than 8 inches in focal length are very few. Most of my photographs have been taken with a $10\frac{1}{2}$-inch Cooke lens adapted for use with a Reflex Korelle camera. For more distant work I use a $24\frac{1}{2}$-inch Ross Zeiss lens which I picked up many years ago in a sale. It must be about forty years old, but its definition even at full aperture is very satisfactory, and is a great tribute to Anglo-German co-operation in the

A Knot (in the foreground) seeks company with Redshanks in the shallows

manufacture of lenses in the early years of this century. The only trouble is that it weighs nearly ten pounds. The method that I use for attaching it to my camera is a source of considerable amusement to my friends. I have a series of home-made telescoping tubes, rather like outsize cocoa tins, which fit into each other and provide the necessary extension with, I fear, a bare minimum of rigidity. When I am in the hide this lens has to rest on a stout horizontal bar which is fixed across the front of the hide and is an essential component of its structure. The camera sits loosely on a large flat table top about 18 inches by 12 which is screwed firmly to the top of a good, solid tripod. The camera can then be swivelled from side to side while the lens remains more or less stationary. I have not perfected any mechanical device for raising and lowering the height of the tripod, but I find that I can adjust the tripod legs speedily enough when the occasion demands it. As this lens is only used for photographing birds that are quite a considerable distance away, a slight increase or decrease in the height of the camera is generally all that is necessary to suit my purpose. A camouflaged lens hood projects out 9 inches in front of the lens. The overall length of this strange-looking apparatus is just over 30 inches from lens hood to camera back—a considerable distance for comfortable manipulation, but it is surprising how effectively one can learn to bring a cumbersome object like this into play when the birds start drawing near. The main trouble arises when it becomes necessary, as it usually does before long, to start photographing from another side of the hide. To withdraw the lens from one 'window' of the hide and insert it in another is a task requiring supreme caution if the birds are not to be alarmed.

The bird photographer who embarks on estuary work soon discovers that he must develop methods very different from those that he has been accustomed to use when interviewing birds at the nest. In nest photography the lens is usually stopped down as far as lighting conditions will allow, and a fairly slow exposure given at a moment when the bird is judged to be still. This method can only be adopted in the estuary occasionally with individual birds or after high tide when the birds are asleep or at rest. But, to my mind, much of the charm of photographing waders at high tide is in attempting to convey the intense vivacity of the scene. Isolated groups may produce better exhibition pictures, but they fail to convey the essence of the occasion, which is one of thronging, crowding, jostling life. High-stepping Redshanks mingle with scurrying Dunlins. Restless Oyster-Catchers keep the smaller waders constantly on the run. As long as the tide is rising there is a spirit of restlessness everywhere, and if you have a score of these lively subjects on the focusing screen at the same time it is simply to invite spoilt negatives to give an exposure of less than a hundredth of a second. But what is not at first realised is the superlative quality of the light out in the estuary on a normally bright day. The depth of focus so essential when birds are scattered over several square yards of beach can only be obtained by stopping the lens down to $f/22$ or beyond, but so brilliant is the light that an exposure of a hundredth of a second on modern fast film will often produce negatives that have a tendency towards over-exposure even at that small stop.

A sunny day in the estuary—if the birds are on the right side of the hide—produces, in my opinion, the ideal conditions under which to work. This is a statement for which I am likely to be criticised severely by most bird photographers, who regard sunshine as a very doubtful ally. There is no doubt that sunshine filtering through overhanging leaves can be an unmitigated nuisance when one is photographing a bird at its nest. Blotches of light and shade play havoc with a bird's plumage in such circumstances, but in the estuary, on the other hand, with predominantly grey birds merging, as Nature

A Turnstone in full breeding-plumage strays amongst the other waders.
On the left, dozing on one leg, is a ruddy-plumaged Knot

intended, into a drab background, a certain amount of contrast is not only desirable but often quite essential if they are not to be paste-board figures on a neutral backcloth. The play of light and shade on their plumage gives them substance, and a glint of sunshine on the sea-washed rocks or on the sea itself gives a sparkle to the picture which it otherwise would lack.

I have described in general terms some of the problems and have hinted at some of the possibilities that await the estuary photographer. It is time to describe in greater detail some of the experiences that await the lone watcher when, by a happy coincidence of tide and weather, he and his quarry are brought together for the high-tide hours. The best way to do this is to give an account of the experiences that befell me when, one lovely August morning, I set off across the mud flats towards the island where I proposed to maroon myself for a six-hour vigil during a period of exceptionally favourable tides. At low ebb, when sand and mud stretched for miles on all sides, the outcrop of sandstone in the estuary on which I proposed to erect my hide was devoid of bird life. A great hummock of rock, looking in the distance like a stranded whale, it seemed to hold little promise of success as I searched its barren surface for a likely place on which to pitch my little tent. Eventually I decided on my site—a flat ledge which commanded a good view of the seaward side of the island—and the tent was soon solidly and firmly established there. A plentiful supply of heavy boulders was at hand, and these were piled all round the edges of the hide, serving the double purpose of weighing down the sacking and adding a convincing touch of camouflage to the structure itself. As yet there was no sign of the incoming tide, but I knew well enough that already it was piling up behind the sand-bars, and would soon come pouring across the flats, flooding gutters and channels and covering the tidal ooze on which the waders were busy feeding. As soon as this happened, birds would be on the wing, speeding across the estuary in search of a resting-place. I disappeared inside the hide long before the first-comers might wish to make a landing on the island's muddy fringe. So much depends on the confidence that can be inspired in these first arrivals. If a few birds decide that it is safe to alight they will act as a magnet, and decoy other birds that are flighting uncertainly over their threatened feeding-grounds. Once the birds have assembled in any strength by the distant water's edge the rising tide will do the rest. This was the happy state of affairs soon after I had settled into my hide. The first arrivals were Oyster-Catchers—a dozen splendidly pied and vermilion birds that lined the island's fringe a hundred yards away. Nothing could have been better, for the brilliance of their plumage in the August sunshine made them a conspicuous sight, and, though they are noisy and vociferous birds, they have a certain dependability of character. They will not panic at the least alarm, and their presence here should have a stabilising influence on the more excitable waders.

Half a dozen Curlews passed overhead, circled the island with some uncertainty, and then came in to alight at the furthermost tip of the sandstone hummock, almost out of sight. Only their heads and incredibly long scimitar bills showed above the ridge of rock behind which they had settled. Then, in twos and threes, and later in parties of a dozen or more, came the Redshanks, agitated as always, and betraying their nervousness by staccato jerkings of heads and tails, and by a great deal of agitated prancing on their high-stilted legs. The presence of other less temperamental waders, however, gave them confidence and they soon settled down to preen and rest. In their grey-and-white livery, with red legs gleaming in the bright sunshine, they made an unforgettable picture.

Meanwhile the tide was steadily rising and the area of the island perceptibly shrinking. Gradually the birds moved nearer, and others began coming in. Scattered groups of Turnstones suddenly appeared on elevated ridges of rock. Some of the adults were still richly plumaged in black, white and tortoiseshell, but young ones of the year were rather scrubby-looking individuals with none of their parents' air of distinction. Agitated Ringed Plovers bobbed and curtsied on the rocks near at hand, and again there was a marked distinction between adults and young. The black gorgets of the young ones were only half-formed, and one could understand how easily they could be confused with Kentish Plovers at this season. The yellowish tinge on

Ringed Plovers mingle with Sanderlings and Dunlins. An immature Ringed Plover is in the middle of the group

their legs put their identity beyond question, for the Kentish Plover in all stages of growth has leaden or blackish legs.

But where were the small folk of the estuary—the Dunlins and Sanderlings? In the distance a smoky mass appeared in the sky. It swayed and swerved this way and that, twisting and turning in a bewildering way as it drew perceptibly nearer. Then overhead there was the sudden rush of a myriad wings: the sky was darkened for a moment as they passed. Three times they circled the island, banking and spiralling as they prepared to land; and then, in a swirling cloud that suddenly rained down a shimmering cascade of birds, they poured down with a dazzling flash of wings and a chorus of thin pipings. There was a momentary hush in the assembled multitude, and then from a thousand throats in unison there broke forth a wonderfully soft piping— almost, one might say, a musical 'purring.' It was the Dunlins' 'sweet jargoning'—a quite enchanting pattern of sound. The island was now a moving carpet of birds. The air was tremulous with their voices. And all the time the area of standing-space was shrinking as the water lapped nearer.

The arrival of a score of gulls brought a mass of small waders scurrying within a few feet of the hide, and one could see now more clearly a semblance of order in the serried ranks of birds that were assembled here. Nearest of all were the smaller waders—Dunlins, Sanderlings, Turnstones and Ringed Plovers, all of them intermingling, and all more or less of a similar size. From time to time a surge of harsh chattering notes came from a group of Turnstones. They seemed less inclined than the others to endure the close proximity of neighbours, but their bellicosity was ' full of sound and fury,

Occasionally a party of Redshanks will swim boldly from one promontory to another

signifying nothing.' Most of the Dunlins retained something of their nuptial finery, but the black smudges on their breasts would soon disappear, and they would don for the winter months a sober, ashy-grey mantle and white under-parts. Some of the Sanderlings had ruddy streaks on their backs, but their breasts were pearly white, and their bills noticeably shorter than the Dunlins'. It was strange to see them comparatively still, for at the tide's edge they are the most restless of all waders, their little twinkling feet always on the move, as they rush hither and thither in pursuit of sandhoppers and other small fry snatched up in the wake of a receding wave.

Behind the small waders the Redshanks had now massed in a company a hundred strong. One small party, crowded out of their original station, swam boldly round the island—a most unusual sight—bobbing up and down in the water like so many miniature ducks—or Phalaropes. The nearest Redshanks were a mere eight yards away, and in this particular group were four Knots that had suddenly and mysteriously arrived in their midst. Shorter of bill and leg, squatter in body and with an entirely distinctive plumage pattern, there could be no mistaking their identity at once.

Flanking the Redshanks on their left were the Oyster-Catchers in a dense phalanx. They, too, had strangers in their midst. A lone Whimbrel alighted

The small waders wisely make way for a Great Black-Backed Gull

by the water's edge, but the press of birds proved distasteful to its solitary disposition, and it did not stay for long. But better things were in store. The attention was suddenly arrested by the arrival of a tall, ruddy-plumaged wader with a bill nearly as long as a Whimbrel's but straight or even slightly up-tilted. It was a Bar-Tailed Godwit still in full breeding-dress. It stood with the Oyster-Catchers—an aristocrat in their midst; and presently, with a nervous flutter of wings, there arrived quite near to the hide an immature bird of the same species with a very slender bill and warm-brown plumage. It stayed for a very short time. The other waders could barely tolerate this

25

Redshanks and a few Dunlins driven nearer the hide

highly strung youngster of the Godwit aristocracy, and it was soon chivied away.

Meanwhile a stampede of small waders from a rocky promontory by the water's edge signified the arrival there of the sinister villain of the estuary—a Great Black-Backed Gull. The Dunlins and Sanderlings wisely gave him a wide berth. The callous look in his eye and the small but wicked hook at the end of his hammer bill are an index to his character. Nothing comes amiss to him and he would have no compunction in disembowelling a small wader should it stray too near. But he is not the only predator that haunts the estuary. Of a sudden a fierce, jarring chatter surged through the Oyster-Catcher host and a deathly hush fell over the rest of the frightened waders. A grey-blue streak flashed past the hide and there alighted on a distant pinnacle of the island a male Peregrine Falcon. There he stood facing the assembled waders, his wings hunched and every line of his compact body threatening murder and sudden death. The Oyster-Catchers were swearing with an intensity that was most impressive, but they did not stir. They knew better than to take to the air with that winged terror in the vicinity, but a trip of Dunlins suddenly dashed off in a panic, and the falcon was after them in a murderous

Redshanks make for the pools and paddle there

flash. From my hide I could not see the end of the incident, but I have no doubt that before long the falcon would be flying in a leisurely manner across the estuary, plucking his victim as he went, and the feathers floating down would be mute evidence of one small wader less in the world.

With the departure of the Peregrine a general feeling of relief pervaded the assembly. Once again the birds began jostling for positions of advantage, and there was a constant stir and movement. Again the surge of wader voices rose and fell, and the blend of their cries, pipings of Dunlins, growlings of

Turnstones, yodelling of Redshanks, yickerings of Oyster-Catchers, made music most wonderful to hear. The tide was now at its height. Congestion on the island had reached its maximum density. There would be no more arrivals now to disturb the peace. The fever of their life was, for the moment, over. Their busy world was hushed. They proceeded to do the obvious and sensible thing—to relax and doze away the high-tide hour. Dunlins and Sanderlings hunched up their little bodies, fluffed out their feathers and snoozed away the time. Most of them were balancing on one leg. All had their

The wardens of the marsh relax. Redshanks dozing after high-tide

beaks tucked well into speckled scapulars. A few beady eyes remained open, but most were closed. The Oyster-Catchers, too, relaxed their vigilance. Orange bills were folded back and tucked out of sight, and white eyelids were drawn across those fiery, watchful eyes. In their orderly platoons and battalions they stood at ease. The far-away mussel beds were submerged and would remain so for another two hours. There was safety in numbers and they could afford to relax. Seen thus in repose the silent multitude harmonised in an unexpected way with the deeply shadowed rock strata on which they had taken their stand.

The Redshanks, too, in spite of their hysterical disposition, were overcome by the prevailing somnolence that now pervaded the scene. Some of them slept, balancing awkwardly on one leg, but others squatted on the warm rocks, where, for all their natural elegance, they looked very like domestic chickens

After high-tide—a mingling of wader species. Turnstones (young one in foreground), Dunlins, Sanderlings and Redshanks move about freely. An intruding Oyster-Catcher is ignored

sunning themselves on a farmyard midden. Having so often suffered from their fussy vigilance on the open marsh, there was a sly satisfaction in photographing the watchdogs of the estuary well and truly off their guard. On this occasion at least they had properly been caught napping.

Turnstones, who never do things by halves, were sprawling about in every attitude of abandoned ease. They reminded one of sleepy tortoiseshell kittens as they lay fluffed out and thoroughly relaxed in the warm sunshine.

After half an hour of slumber during which hardly a sound came from the thousand birds assembled here, a subtle change came over the sleeping community. A soft piping began to spread through the flock. It was the signal to awaken. The tide had begun to ebb, and the birds were beginning to get restive. Soon they were thoroughly awake and ready for a period of social intercourse. From now onwards there was a constant stirring and changing of places. A restless Oyster-Catcher came wandering amongst the smaller waders and they no longer shied away at its approach. One or two Redshanks strayed away from the main flock and took to paddling in the shallow pools left by the receding waters. The Dunlins also made for these pools, and there they splashed about and preened themselves for the next half-hour. Then began a steady trickle of birds away to the newly exposed mud flats and sand banks. The small waders went first, but the Oyster-Catchers and Redshanks were not slow to follow them. The assembly gradually disintegrated, but long after the main body had departed there were still some that were reluctant to leave. And little wonder if they had only just completed their vast migratory flight to these shores. They needed rest if they were to recover from their fatigue, and gain strength for the next lap of their equatorial journey.

Four hours in the hide had cramped my limbs and it was time to emerge. As I staggered out, the few remaining birds sped hastily away. Another hour must pass before I could retrace my steps to the mainland, but a bird photographer also needs relaxation after an experience such as this. Across the gleaming sands the small waders in their hundreds were busily questing for food, trilling to one another happily as they dibbled in the soft mud. I, too, lying in comfort on the warm rocks in the sunshine, was possessed with great happiness and a feeling of quite extraordinary privilege. As intimate companions on a sea-girt rock I had had a multitude of Nature's shyest and most elusive creatures. Not to many is it given to dwell thus for a magic hour with a host of Ariels on an enchanted island when the tide is high.

3
A High Tide at Midnight

OCTOBER in the estuary is a month of variable fortune for the wader enthusiast. The big battalions of August and September have passed through, but there is always the chance that some belated host may arrive overnight to swell the numbers of those that have already taken up winter quarters there. A stability is already noticeable in the numbers of Dunlins and Sanderlings which flock into the island at high tide. Even the volatile Redshanks have a more sedentary look about them, and, along the high tide-line, Turnstones—a fairly constant number now—heave and shove their way through the tangles of seaweed that lie rotting there. A few Purple Sandpipers are scattered over the rocky shores of the islets, and already show by the regularity with which they frequent the same locality that they have settled in for the winter. A score of Bar-Tailed Godwits work over the mud flats at low water, plunging their bills up to the hilt in the succulent mud, and forgathering with their kind when driven from the tidal ooze by the incoming flood. The flocks of Knots are an unpredictable factor at this season. Sometimes there are mere hundreds: at other times, numberless thousands. Nesting the farthest north of all our waders, they show less inclination than the rest of their kindred to quit our shores at the first approach of winter. October is also the best month for Curlews. Here they find temporary refuge before flying westwards to the Irish mosses where so many of them will pass the winter months.

But dominating all other birds of the estuary at this time of the year—as indeed through all the winter months—are the Oyster-Catchers. Their autumn assemblage is nearing completion. When they mass together at high tide, a noisy, colourful harlequinade of excitable birds, their numbers are almost beyond computation.

To my mind there are few experiences more wholly satisfying to one who has been starved of winged company than to lie concealed for an hour or two in their midst; to be engulfed by multitudes of pied and coral birds. As they mass together in their serried ranks on the island's shelving rocks one can detect an orderliness about their manœuvres. There is a nice precision in their spacing, and a definite tendency to form up in 'line abreast,' social

31

Part of the vast autumn Oyster-Catcher assembly in the Cheshire Dee

traits one is surprised to find in a bird of such individual character as the Oyster-Catcher.

The regularity with which they used a particular island roost suggested the intriguing possibility of spending a night in their company some time in October when tides would be favourable with high water at midnight, and the absence of a moon to favour the project of stalking about amongst them in the darkness.

My brother expressed a willingness to accompany me on this unorthodox venture, and together we crossed the mud flats as a blustery autumn day drew to its close. In a secluded corner on the island we pitched our little sleeping tent where overhanging shelves of rock afforded some shelter from the prevailing wind. We had both of us had an exhausting day in the estuary, and were more than ready to take a few hours' rest before the oncoming tide brought in the birds. We settled into our blankets and prepared for sleep. From out on the muddy waste that surrounded us the trill of small waders came as a reminder that the gathering darkness would bring but little interruption to them in their incessant quest for food. An occasional Curlew flew skirling overhead, and half a mile away, at the edge of the tide, the distant cries of Oyster-Catchers told of mussel beds that were already flooding, and of birds that were being driven slowly but relentlessly from their feeding-grounds. It was a pleasant background for sleep, and it was not long before we were both lulled into oblivion.

Some three hours later we came back to consciousness, aware of a quite extraordinary, all-penetrating clamour dinning into our ears and pervading and dominating our little island kingdom. The Oyster-Catchers had arrived

32

A sleepy Redshank who preferred the company of Dunlins for the rest hour

and were already crowding in on us. Cautiously we opened a flap at the front of the tent and peered outside. It was nearing midnight, but out here in the estuary it was by no means wholly dark. Low clouds in the sky reflected a glow from the coastal towns that fringed the estuary, and gave enough illumination for us to see that Oyster-Catchers in scores—in hundreds—were now surrounding us, all of them piping at the tops of their voices. The nearest were not more than five yards away: the sleeping tent quite clearly held no fears for them at all. As we lay watching them, a couple of birds came trotting up almost to our faces. I feel sure that had the front of the tent been wide open we should have had them walking right inside. In the darkness their white breasts and underparts had an almost luminous quality, but it was not until they mounted the rocky ledges above the tent and were silhouetted against the night sky that their heads and bills showed clearly.

And all the while, above the surge of the sea and the whistling of wind over bare rocks, came the clamour of their voices; a cacophony of yicker-

33

ing cries, of kleepings and pipings and yelpings; a splendid confusion of tumultuous sound; a midnight symphony of music wild and exciting which had a stimulating effect on us such as we had never experienced before.

We had brought with us on this midnight expedition a camera and an independent flashlight apparatus. Armed with these, we began a stealthy crawl through the Oyster-Catcher host towards some rocky platforms by the water's edge which we had noted before dark were suitable for photographic purposes. I must confess that my immediate ambition had nothing to do with photography. I dearly wanted to touch an Oyster-Catcher in the dark. But we were soon to discover that these birds could see at least as well as us— probably, I suspect, a little better. They kept flipping away three or four yards ahead of us as we crawled along, and my ambition was not realised.

The first flash set up an alarming clamour from the birds, and some of them fled in panic. The second flash was a complete disaster. The bulb exploded with a loud report and showered flaming magnesium on to the rocks which a moment before had held a dozen unsuspecting birds. It took them some time to recover from this alarming display, and, as we resumed our prowlings, we sensed a spirit of restlessness abroad. The next flash—the only one that produced a picture of any worth at all—was to be the last, not because the Oyster-Catchers were particularly disturbed by it, but because the flashlight apparatus broke down, and no amount of coaxing would induce it to work again. It was not really surprising considering the conditions under which it was being used. The wind was now whipping salt spray over the island, and blown sand, insidious and penetrating, was being hurled at us with a violence that caused acute discomfort wherever it met our exposed flesh.

So we abandoned any further attempts at photography, and contented ourselves with the joy of stalking groups of birds on the more sheltered ledges of the island. We retain many pleasant memories of that remarkable hour spent, for the most part, in a creeping posture on the shelving rocks. We discovered that a flock of Herring Gulls also used the island as a roost, and, disturbed by our presence, they hovered in ominous silence above our heads. It was an eerie sensation to look up and see, silhouetted darkly against the night sky, the figure of an enormous bird suspended menacingly a few feet above one's head. They came as near as they dared in the darkness, and their silent presence lent a sinister touch to the night's adventures.

The hour of the high tide, when the birds were compelled to endure our presence, all too quickly passed. As soon as the outlying reefs were exposed by

34

the ebbing waters, the uneasy birds moved away in increasing numbers until the island was deserted. We retired to our tent and to well-earned rest.

Viewed in the cold light of morning, with rain slanting down over the estuary, and with all our apparatus damp and sand-ridden, the experiences of the midnight hour seemed unreal, and, it must be confessed, rather pointless. But later on, in retrospect, we felt it had been well worth while. It is an experience that we intend to repeat before long, with more efficient flashlight apparatus and under better weather conditions. Photographically it might well produce most interesting results.

Waders on the island pay little heed to passing craft

4

A January Tide on the Cheshire Dee

SEVEN o'clock on a dark and raw January morning, with snow, driven before a searching north-westerly wind, sweeping across the countryside, obliterating familiar landmarks and muffling the sound of my footsteps as I plodded down the coastal road and across the golf links towards the estuary—a most unpromising setting for an expedition of this kind, and yet—who knows? Today, one of the highest tides of the winter would flood the estuary. This weather should bring the birds very close, though the chances of photography were slender indeed. But first, the island must be discovered. Somewhere in the darkness a mile away across the mud flats was that low sandstone hummock which was my objective. Beyond it, over the distant mussel beds, the tide was already creeping in. There was no time to be lost if the intervening creeks were to be crossed dry-shod.

Striking out across the desolate waste of mud, I found the line of sand dunes behind me had disappeared before I had gone a hundred yards. There was nothing for it but to press on blindly. Past and future had ceased to exist. The present was all that mattered, and the urgency of keeping my sense of direction in the confusion of swirling snow. It would be all too easy to bear off to the right or left in the first arc of a circle that would eventually lure me onwards to the edge of that ' cruel crawling foam ' which, as every school-boy knows, brought Mary to her watery grave when she went to call the cattle home across these self-same sands of Dee—a chilling thought for a January dawn. Across the murky, snow-laden sky a leaden pallor was creeping, bring-ing with it a measure of comfort, for surely with daybreak approaching the island's shape would soon be visible. Yes, in a momentary lull in the blizzard, there was its familiar hump showing darkly against the horizon, still a quarter of a mile away and far to the left of where I had been heading, but immeasur-ably reassuring for all that.

Burdened as I was with layer upon layer of clothing and a rucksack full of photographic gear, I broke into a run, for time was pressing. Across the flats I slithered and squelched, and reached the intervening creek just as the froth which precedes the full tidal flow came rounding the corner fifty yards away: I was only just in time. With a floundering leap I crossed this final obstacle and stood on solid ground once more. Another few minutes and the widening channel would have been impassable. It was a very near thing, and I sat down for a few moments to regain my breath, filled with a sense of exaltation and relief, and glowing with that particular brand of satisfaction which is the daily experience of those incurably optimistic souls who leap into the morning train just as it steams out of the station.

But here was no cushioned comfort of a railway carriage in which to relax. A hide had to be constructed without delay, and the materials had to be discovered on the island itself, for I had brought a bare minimum of equipment with me—a groundsheet on which to lie, and a square of sacking for shelter from above. A quantity of driftwood was soon collected, and an old lobster pot, discovered amongst the tide-wrack, was speedily requisitioned. Large boulders of sandstone were piled on the edges of the groundsheet. Spars of driftwood made a framework for the roof, and the lobster pot gave it a little additional height at the front. Over this primitive structure the sacking was stretched, and secured from flapping by an additional layer of stones. Finally, snow was piled against the sides and sprinkled over the roof, and I was able to crawl within, steaming from my exertions, as the first Oyster-Catchers began to assemble along the edge of the tide a couple of hundred yards away. Though my igloo was sadly lacking in comfort, at least I had the satisfaction of knowing that it matched its surroundings to perfection.

For the next ten minutes I was too busy disposing my apparatus within the hide to pay much attention to the incoming birds, though I could tell by the increasing volume of sound that things were happening in a big way. When next I peered through a chink between the sandstone blocks it was to discover that the full weight of the blizzard had broken over the estuary in all its fury. Visibility was down to fifty yards, and the birds, hastening off the exposed flats, were crowding in on all sides of the island. Already the nearest were a mere dozen yards away, and more were arriving at every moment. Pressing in on each other as they manoeuvred for the more sheltered ledges, the clamour they were making was indescribable. Oyster-Catchers outnumbered all other species, but Curlews, Bar-Tailed Godwits, Redshanks and Knots were all there in force. Soon the nearest Oyster-Catchers were packing together within half a dozen yards of the hide. Facing into the wind and treading uncomfortably on the snow, they seemed reluctant to relax and doze as is their usual wont. They poked about uneasily at the snow with their orange, pick-axe bills. To many of them it must have been their first experience of this cold and unfamiliar substance. It was clearly an experience they did not relish. As they shifted their positions in the flock, ' leap-frogging '

Oyster-Catchers swim quite readily when so inclined

over their neighbours away from the advancing tide, I noticed many birds that flew with one leg trailing down and the other completely hidden from view. At first I thought there must be an unusually large number of cripples in the flock—birds that had lost a leg but had survived, as they will, in spite of this handicap. This impression was strengthened when, again and again, I saw these one-legged birds alight on their one sound leg, hopping a few paces unsteadily before coming to a halt. Only by close observation of a few individuals behaving in this way was I finally convinced of the true state of affairs. A bird in danger of overbalancing when jostled by its neighbour would soon produce its missing limb. But, for preference, the spare leg was tucked away quite out of sight. To use one leg for standing in the snow was an unfortunate necessity. But why expose the other?

When the worst of the storm blew over and visibility improved, it was possible to obtain a rough approximation of the total numbers in this vast concourse. I ran my eye over the assembly, and, computing in multiples of a hundred and checking my figures as carefully as I could, I was forced to the conclusion that the Oyster-Catchers alone numbered eight thousand. A score of Curlews and twice as many Godwits clung to the outer fringes of the multitude. The Redshanks were bolder, and one small party had moved in for shelter quite near to me, where some Dunlins—a mere handful compared with their numbers here in early autumn—had taken their stand. A few Purple Sandpipers were there too, portly little waders with smoky, dull

Dunlins: a study in reflections

plumage and yellow legs. A dozen Turnstones, soberly apparelled at this season of the year, huddled with them. But though the smaller waders as a whole were not plentiful, their deficiency in numbers was more than made up by the astonishing number of Knots that came streaming in. With a mighty rush of wings, a great host of them came hurtling towards the island, cleaving the eddying snowflakes with the impact of their bodies as, in dense formation, they swept past the hide, circled, and returned once more in a determined effort to effect a landing. There was little standing room left, but a small gap in the Oyster-Catcher ranks was discovered, and, as if pouring through a narrow funnel, a whole nation of Knots streamed down from above, widening

D

the wedge they had started, and, packing together head to tail and shoulder to shoulder, they created in a few moments a solid carpet of grey in the midst of the pied and orange-scarlet Oyster-Catcher host. There they stayed until a flotilla of Gulls—Herring and Common in about equal numbers, with here and there a squalling Black Head—decided to come ashore, causing the entire company to stampede into the air before alighting again a safe fifty yards away.

Out to sea a black line of duck had been moving nearer, carried hither by the set of the tide, and it was possible now to distinguish them as individuals. They were Scoters, four score of them, bobbing and plunging in the tideway. Nearer at hand were half a dozen Wigeon, and one drake in splendid plumage came swimming past within a few yards of the hide.

The snow was now falling intermittently, and clearer patches of sky were beginning to show. Soon the light might improve sufficiently to give reasonable chances of photographic success. But meanwhile a numbness was creeping over my limbs. I was beginning to wonder how much longer I could endure the discomfort of lying prone on these cold, hard rocks. In an effort to restore circulation to one of my legs I tried cautiously doubling it beneath my body. Instantly the most appalling cramp seized me, and in one sudden, agonised plunge, my foot shot clean through the wall of the hide, toppling the boulders in all directions with the most devastating effect on the assembled birds. With a roar of wings and a babel of astonished cries, the whole host leapt into the air. I struggled upright in the wreckage, thrust aside the sacking roof, and enjoyed to the full the indescribably moving spectacle of ten thousand birds suddenly and simultaneously taking to the air, filling the skies with their wild clamour before streaming away, as they did too soon, to the security of another island lower down the estuary.

From past experience I knew it was useless to attempt to rebuild the hide in the hope that some of them might return; besides which, I was chilled and stiff and in urgent need of exercise and warmth.

A pile of driftwood was soon collected in a sheltered spot. It was damp and at first it stubbornly resisted my attempts at kindling a fire, but after a while it relented, and soon I had a merry blaze to thaw my limbs and dry my outer garments.

No doubt a mile away across the receding waters there were people on the shore who, peering through the curtain of snowflakes and seeing my column of smoke out on the island, would be shaking their heads at the lunacy of one who had chosen this of all days for marooning himself out in the estuary.

In self-defence I would maintain, with Hamlet, that madness of this kind is largely conditioned by the direction of the prevailing wind.

> I am but mad north north west.
> When the wind is southerly I can tell a hawk from a handsaw.

The luck of the compass plays a large part in the comforts or discomforts of the estuary. One should not limit one's tidal experiences to days when the wind blows softly from the south. Today it had blown most fittingly and whole-heartedly from the north—from those barren, arctic regions where so many of these waders had been cradled. For a brief hour on this island I had shared with them the discomforts of the storm. Their near and confiding presence had more than compensated me for the rigours of the day. Perhaps I was a little mad, but madness, as Hamlet discovered, has compensations. Today my heaven and earth had been most amply filled with winged company. An island prince, with a store of sweet memories, I had no further need for flights of angels to sing me to my rest.

5

March—In Quest of the Grey Plover

DURING the month of March a subtle change comes over many of the estuary birds. Redshanks will suddenly break off from feeding, and, with mincing steps and high-arched wings, begin cavorting round each other in the first stages of their elaborate courtship. The bubbling cry of the Curlew is heard over the green marsh by day, and at night the mournful calls of birds already on the move rain down from the quiet skies. Here and there in the flocks of Dunlins is a bird with dusky underparts. Soon all will be donning the handsome, black waistcoat which is their nuptial dress. In a short time now, Redshanks, Curlews and Dunlins will be leaving the estuary and dispersing inland over marsh and moorland breeding haunts. Already on the shingle banks Ringed Plovers have taken up their territories. On sunny days their time is spent in amorous pursuit, and ' scrapes ' are being made amongst the pebbles. In the last week of March the Lapwings in the water meadows begin to make their nests. Already in a near-by copse a Woodcock crouches over her half-incubated eggs.

But though the sweet restlessness of spring affects the resident species to a marked degree, the northern-nesting waders that have wintered in the estuary —the Godwits, Turnstones, Knots and many others—still show no signs of change in dress or disposition. There is no need yet for them to get excited at the thought of spring. The barren tundras where they nest are still imprisoned in the iron grip of the arctic winter. Many weeks must pass before their northward journey can begin. April will pass and most of May before they receive the distant summons. Then, their numbers strengthened by arrivals from more southerly shores, they take their departure, drawn as by an invisible magnet northwards to the land of the midnight sun. Belated stragglers will still be passing through in June, and yet the marvel of it is that by the middle of July the return migration will have started, and the first few tired birds will be seen resting on our coasts before proceeding onwards as they journey to the south. Six weeks of the arctic summer allow them sufficient time to fulfil their whole, intensive breeding cycle. Courtship, nest-building, egg-laying and incubation, the fledging of downy young, all is achieved in this brief period of time. This alone is a remarkable feat, but add to this the miracle of their

A winter flock of Grey Plovers in a south coast estuary

migratory flights—from Britain alone a journey each way of some two thousand miles—and 'still the wonder grows'!

Of the many waders that use the estuary as a temporary refuge when winging to and from their distant breeding-grounds, none has for me a greater fascination than the Grey or Silver Plover. To do him equal justice, his name, like his dress, should vary with the season. In winter no birds can show a greater harmony of subtle shades of grey. In summer he is all contrast—black as jet is his throat and breast, and his back is a glory of spangled silver. One of the last of the waders to disclose the secret of its nesting haunts, even today the extent of those haunts is not fully known. In 1875, near the mouth of the Petchora River, Seebohm and Harvie-Brown found the first authenticated eggs in Siberian Europe. Others, since then, have discovered further haunts of this tundra-loving bird, but nowhere is it found in any numbers, and there still remain vast tracts of land to be explored.

The same elusive qualities that give this bird an enviable reputation on its breeding-grounds also distinguish it on its visits to the estuary. It is the despair of the tide-line photographer, not because it is abnormally shy, but because it seldom yields to the persuasion of the tide as most of the waders will. There are, besides, but few estuaries in Britain which have their resident winter flocks. To succeed with the Grey Plover you must live in the south.

In *A Book of British Waders*—Brian Vesey-Fitzgerald's delightful contribution to wader literature—under a photograph of Grey Plovers taken in the waders' aviary at the Zoological Gardens in Regent's Park, the author put these words: ' The Grey Plover is another bird that is very rarely photographed.

43

I do not know that it has ever been photographed in the wild by an Englishman.'

To the casual reader that might well be taken as a simple statement of fact. To the tide-line photographer it was a definite challenge. I vowed that one day I would secure a portrait of this most elusive bird! But the war years intervened, and the Grey Plovers had, beside their own inherent wariness, the additional security of man-made coastal barricades to shield them. Screened by anti-tank erections and by mile upon mile of barbed wire, they fed serenely out on the tidal ooze, secure from fowlers and photographers alike.

When the war was over and the barricades removed, the problem of how to induce Grey Plovers to come within photographic range still remained. One could view them through glasses a hundred yards away out on the mud flats often enough during the spring and autumn migrations, but the camera can only operate at a tenth of that distance, and it is useless to try and stalk them there. With camera held in readiness I have tried approaching them cautiously across the Norfolk sands where, in August, birds still apparelled in their glorious black and silver livery may frequently be encountered. But never have I succeeded in getting within even distant photographic range. In the north-western estuaries where I served my apprenticeship in the craft of 'wait and see' photography the Grey Plover was a comparatively rare visitor, and few, if any, stayed to winter there. But on the South Coast, over the vast expanse of tidal mud in Chichester, Langstone and Portsmouth Harbours, a considerable number—many hundreds in all—take up their permanent winter quarters, and, when the tide is high, resort with Godwits and Oyster-Catchers to shingle reefs or grassy islets, or, not infrequently, rush in headlong flight from island to island during the brief hours in which they are driven from their feeding-grounds. From a bird photographer's point of view the fault of these great estuaries is not the lack of islands where the birds may rest, but their over-abundance. It is quite useless to erect a hide on one island when there is another equally attractive one half a mile away. You may well find yourself sitting out a seven-hour vigil without a bird in sight.

The only hope of interviewing Grey Plovers was to find a secluded bay or harbour with a solitary reef to which they might resort. After many fruitless expeditions, an island full of promise was eventually found, but there were many difficulties to be overcome. To begin with, the island—a narrow shingle ridge—was tenable only at moderately high tides. In the words of a local fowler: " In full moon tides I reckon she goes right under." He was right, as I found to my extreme discomfiture on my first expedition there.

44

Grey Plovers, Bar-Tailed Godwits and a Knot relax together at high-tide

To view the birds at a correct angle and with the sun not shining directly into the camera lens, it was necessary to place the hide in such a way that one would inevitably be up to the knees in water at high tide; that is unless one built a shingle mound of huge proportions, a task more suitable for a mechanical excavator than for bare hands and a shovel. This elementary fact was not appreciated on the first occasion there. The tide arrived before the birds, and when the water came surging across the stones on which my companion and I were crouching in a small 'sitting' hide, there was no alternative but to scramble out ingloriously and take refuge on all that was left of the island— a few square yards of shingle at its highest point. Viewed from the mainland half a mile away, the sight of two photographers and the remains of their tent, perched on a shingle spit a few inches above the surrounding watery wastes, must have been quite amusing, if not alarming, but fortunately the beach was deserted, and no boats set out to effect a dramatic but quite unnecessary rescue. When, four hours later, we were able to recross the creek that separated us from the mainland, we were already laying plans for a second expedition in a few days' time when the tide would not be quite so high.

This time a mound of shingle was raised on which the tent, now built high enough for standing room, was solidly installed. Pockets to hold shingle and sand had been stitched to the sides, for in this way one can overcome that insidious enemy of bird photographers—flapping canvas. After due preparations had been made, I crawled inside, and my companion heaped shingle round the sides of the hide until the canvas was as tight as a drum and the wooden supports creaked under the strain. He then withdrew and crossed over to the mainland, and I settled down for a lengthy wait. High tide was at 1 p.m. It was now about half-past-ten. Twenty minutes later, just as I had finished my photographic preparations and was settling down for a sandwich lunch, there was a rending crash above my head. With a splintering of wood and a tearing of canvas the whole hide collapsed inwards. The weight of the shingle had proved too much. Three of the uprights had given way, reducing the height of the hide almost by half, and the whole structure had slewed round into the shape of a compressed lozenge. It was a bitter blow, but the tide was already coming up the channel and my companion was out of reach. I had to make the best of it. Tightening the loosened canvas as best I could, half-kneeling, half-stooping, I awaited the coming of the birds.

It was not long before the first Dunlins came flickering in to settle on the shingle by the island's edge. They were quickly joined by a score of Turnstones who poked about amongst the seaweeds and were reluctantly forced higher up the shelving bank with each succeeding wave. A few Ringed Plovers, restless as always, made little stooping runs amongst the grey pebbles, preferring to run hither and thither where the fancy took them, rather than to settle down for relaxation with the somnolent Dunlins. Then, from across the estuary, came the sound I had been waiting for—the high, musical whistle of Grey Plovers on the wing. Three dozen strong they came, sweeping past the hide, circling the island hesitantly, and then, reassured by the presence of smaller waders, down they came, alighting in the furthermost shallows. There, standing head to wind, they made a most impressive sight. Soon, alighting in their midst, came half a dozen Bar-Tailed Godwits, and then, vociferous as always, a score of Oyster-Catchers to form a pleasing pattern of black, white and scarlet behind them. The tide came creeping in across the shingles and they were all kept on the move, making short flights over each other as they sought the shallower water in front. Nearer and nearer they came until the main body was only twenty yards away. For the last ten minutes I had been anxiously watching the weather. The sky had been darkening. A thin drizzle of rain now rustled against the canvas of the hide. The light was desperately poor for this kind of work, but it was now or never, for the water in the hide was now above my ankles, and, in my crouching position, if it came much higher I should have no option but to use the knife I had open in readiness for slashing the canvas and making good my escape. It was not so much the thought of a temporary wetting that weighed with me, but the knowledge that whatever happened I was marooned on the island for another four hours, and to sit for that length of time in sodden clothing in the month of March was simply to invite trouble.

So in spite of the appalling light I had to get my pictures without delay.

46

The concentration of waders was a major difficulty. Much as I would have liked strings of individual birds on the water's edge, it was just impossible to separate them. Oyster-Catchers, Godwits, Grey Plovers, and, here and there, a bunch of Knots, were all intermingled. Nearer at hand the Dunlins and Turnstones had been compressed into a tight company on a dozen square yards of shingle. Already many of them appeared to be sound asleep. But the Oyster-Catchers and Grey Plovers were very much alert, eyeing the hide with the gravest suspicion, and shifting about uneasily on the flooded pebbles. The Godwits, like the smaller waders, appeared possessed with one idea only—to find congenial company and immediately to sleep. No sooner had they moved a yard or two than those incredibly long bills of theirs were

Bar-Tailed Godwits with Grey Plovers and Oyster-Catchers at the edge of the tide

folded back and buried deep within their scapulars, and, to all intents and purposes, they were asleep. Accurate focusing on this mixed company, spread in depth over several yards of shallow water, was a difficult procedure, but somehow I managed to take a dozen photographs in half as many minutes before I made a fatal slip. The camera lens was swung too rapidly towards some new arrivals. The alarm was given, and in a flash the island was swept clean of birds. In swirling clouds they streamed across to the mainland and began to settle on the shingles there. This, I thought, is the end of photography for today, and I considered the advisability of escaping from the hide without further delay; but on inspecting a measuring rod I had planted nearby, up which the water level had been steadily rising for the last half-hour, I saw to my relief that the tide had turned. In a short time the water would drain away from my feet and I should be standing on dry land again. It was worth waiting on the distant chance that some of the birds might return. Meanwhile my companion on the mainland, realising the situation, was preparing to act as a beater in an effort to speed back the birds to me. I saw him approach the assembled flock and put them up: but they flew over his head and alighted a quarter of a mile further along the beach. Again he repeated the manœuvre, this time with more success. The smaller waders came streaming back to the island with one or two Oyster-Catchers, Grey Plovers

A group of Turnstones and two Knots on a raised shingle-mound

and Knots with them, but the greater part of the larger birds flew steadily across the estuary and disappeared on the shore a mile or more away. A shingle ridge by the water's edge proved an irresistible attraction to a returning party of Turnstones, and two Knots, mounting the ridge with them, made an attractive picture as they stood outlined against the sea. A solitary Grey Plover also stood obligingly in shallow water within photographic range, and presently the other waders grouped around it, and there they stood and dozed whilst the ebbing waters receded from the estuary. A gleam of late afternoon sun came through the clouds and shone warmly on their little hunched-up bodies. The Grey Plover dozed too, but with head held forward, unlike the other waders whose heads had all disappeared as they folded their beaks into the feathers on their mottled backs. For half an hour I let them slumber in peace, and then decided I could endure my cramped quarters no longer.

I cut a slit through the back of the hide and crawled out. Although they were only twenty yards away, the resting birds did not see me, and I lay for some time stretched out in comfort in the shadow of the hide. After a while the twitterings of Dunlins and the bellicose growlings of Turnstones told me that the sleeping host was awakening. Slowly I stood up and showed myself. Even then they were reluctant to leave, but as I moved forward they all took

A gleam of late afternoon sun shines warmly on the hunched-up bodies of the sleeping waders. The Grey Plover is the only bird in the group that dozes with head held forward

to the air, separating out into species as they departed with a rush of wings and a chorus of thin pipings.

It had been a memorable day, and although for another two hours I must pace the length and breadth of my ever-widening island to keep away the cold, my heart was warm within me. At long last I had kept my rendezvous with the Grey Plover, and, in spite of poor light and adverse conditions, the spools of film that nestled in my pocket were evidence of a challenge that had been met, and of a day of days most profitably spent.

6

The Estuary in May

TO anyone who is not familiar with the vagaries of the wader tribes, May would seem to be a most unpromising month for waiting out in the estuary on the off-chance of seeing what may turn up with the tide. Inland, the season is well advanced. The hedgerows are white with hawthorn blossom and lilac is in bloom. Many of the garden birds have fledged their early broods. Starlings, Tits and Nuthatches are feeding half-grown young. In brake and coppice where the bluebells are already past their prime the migrant warblers have all staked out their territorial claims, and nesting activity is in full swing. Indeed, for many birds the short, intensive season when they reproduce their kind is already nearing its completion. Why, then, waste one's time sitting out a tide in the estuary when the resident waders that have wintered there are known to be dispersed and scattered in their breeding-haunts on mountain, moor and marsh? Surely it is likely to be a complete waste of energy and time.

But the wader enthusiast knows that May can be, in many ways, the most exciting month of all. It is true that our resident waders are mostly scattered far and wide, and some already blessed with eggs or young. But what about the northern migrants? It may be that we in this country are experiencing an early heat-wave with temperatures up in the seventies. But what about the North Lands? It is hard to realise, as we luxuriate in the warmth of a premature English summer, that the sub-polar regions where so many of the northern waders have their nesting-haunts are still in the grip of the arctic winter. These distant travellers, in obedience to the deepest instincts of their race, delay their northward passage until, with dramatic haste, the late arctic spring awakens to teeming life the insect population of those mosquito-ridden lands, and the fast-melting snows lay bare the seeds and berries that have, for the last nine months, been lying hidden there.

It is in May that many of these northern-nesting waders pass along our shores in strength. It is then that one can often see them in the full glory of their breeding dress. There is a great element of chance about the species that may be encountered, but this only adds to the fascination of the pursuit. The day may be rich in experience: it may be a total blank. But whether the birds are there or not, the setting is always delightful. One can dream away the noonday hours on an island in mid-May as profitably as anywhere else in the kingdom.

But as the purpose of this chapter is to persuade those who would not otherwise consider the project to risk for themselves the uncertainty of a May day in the estuary, I shall not dwell on the possible disappointments that may attend them at this season of the year, but limit my narrative to the experiences of a day when the fates were kind to me. I have not had enough May days in the estuary to know whether my good fortune on this particular occasion was exceptional. I see no reason why it should have been. The only way of finding out is to go again next year—and the year after—as I fully intend to do.

Much of my tidal experience has been gained in what the bird-photographer usually reckons as the 'off-season' months—autumn, winter and early spring. To find oneself setting off down the sea road towards the estuary on a flawless morning in mid-May, with the scent of hawthorn heavy on the air, had about it a touch of unreality. What business had I to be heading for the island at the height of the nesting season?

As if to confirm my doubts, a pair of Lapwings in the field I had to cross were tumbling through the air and crying out their protests for all the world to hear. Their eggs hatched out a week ago, and four young Lapwings were playing hide and seek amongst the buttercups that clothed the meadow in a cloth of gold. A Song Thrush flew past, her beak cramful of worms. Those spotted youngsters of hers were now out of the nest and lurking in the cover of a hedgerow bank. From half a mile away across the low-lying marshland came the sweet yodelling of nesting Redshanks. Their eggs were now hard-set, and soon those liquid calls of theirs would change to agitated clamour when their downy young were running in the marsh.

Where the grassland ended abruptly at the shingle bank another note was heard—the anxious 'toorli' call of a Ringed Plover as she slipped away across the beach. A fortnight ago I had found her nest, a shallow 'scrape' amongst the pebbles. Now it was empty. Only a few tiny fragments of egg-shell were there to explain that the cause of her anxiety today was not her eggs but those four little chicks that were hiding somewhere amongst the pebbles on the open beach. There was no time to search for them now, for already the tide was creeping past the harbour bar and soon the intervening creek would fill.

From high up in the blue sky overhead came the 'scaar . . . scaar . . .' cries of the newly arrived Little Terns. For the next three months they would be here to charm the eye and gladden the ear. Would that these shingle banks

51

on which they nested could be made into a sanctuary where they would be safe from those human magpies who yearly robbed them of their eggs. A few more years of thoughtless persecution and this colony, like many another, would be faced with extinction.

As the last few yards of the beach were crossed, from the weedy fringe of the channel that separated the shingle banks from the mud flats came the jarring chatter of a number of small waders that were foraging there—Turnstones, of course, quarrelsome as always, but what a change had taken place in their appearance since that blustery March day when last I saw them on this same weed-strewn shore. The 'Tortoiseshell Plovers' were now resplendent in full breeding-plumage, most strikingly handsome birds with chestnut upper parts boldly chequered with black and white, and with a colour pattern on their heads that gave them a comical, bespectacled appearance. It is hard to believe that such striking plumage can have any protective value, yet in their nesting haunts on the barren, stony islands of the north they are said to be uncommonly difficult to see.

On reaching the island on which I intended to secrete myself for the next five hours, I found that sufficient of the shingle mound I had erected there in March was left to serve my present purposes. Today I planned to build my hide with particular care, for, with the approach of the nesting season and the stimulus that the breeding impulse gives to a bird's already mercurial disposition, it would be necessary to take extra precautions. If any birds came to the island today they would not be winter residents for whom resorting here at high tide had become a familar custom. They would be transient visitors to the estuary; casual wanderers who had dropped in for a few hours; restless spirits, who, but for the vagaries of wind and weather, might well be several hundred miles to the north or south of here.

Instead of a sacking hide of comfortable proportions, a different structure had to be devised. First, the shingle mound was raised, by dint of strenuous digging, by an extra couple of feet. Then, inside the mound, a hollow sufficiently large to accommodate photographer and apparatus was scooped. On top of this a framework of interlacing canes was placed, and a groundsheet tightly stretched above. A further layer of shingle round its edge made all secure. Lastly, to add the final touch, seaweed was plentifully strewn on top and sides. An abundance of this most useful hide material was readily obtainable along the high-tide line, and it was whilst plying to and fro with armfuls of rotting weed that my eye suddenly caught sight of a neat little hollow in the shingle in which reposed the four eggs—black-freckled on a stone-grey ground colour—of a Ringed Plover. Their points were all turned inwards in true Plover fashion, and they were still faintly warm, though there had been no sign of the parent birds since I had arrived on the island half an hour ago. The nest was only twenty yards from my hide, but much as I regretted the inconvenience caused to the parents by my invasion of their nesting quarters, I felt I could hardly take the blame for intruding thus innocently on their privacy.

But not wishing to prolong their anxiety longer than was absolutely necessary, I finished my preparations with all speed and retired within my shingle mound. It was not long before both parents came flying in from the mud flats, and, whilst the male stood on guard, the female began a series of

Ringed Plover in a setting which harmonises with the bird's bold plumage-pattern

long stooping runs which eventually brought her to the nest. Out fluffed her brooding feathers, and down she sank, almost out of sight, a dumpy little figure sitting unobtrusively amongst the pebbles.

By now the tide was running well and the channels on either side of the island were filling. Birds were on the wing, and it was not long before a small party of Turnstones came flying in to alight quite near the hide. They were the first to seek out the island as a resting-place, but for the present they spent their time in true Turnstone fashion, heaving away at the pebbles and snatching up sandhoppers that were lurking beneath. A trip of Dunlins soon alighted fifty yards away at the water's edge. Were they of the northern or the southern race? They are indistinguishable in the field, and as the migrations of the two sub-species overlap one can never be certain. But at this late date our resident southern birds would mostly be dispersed over the mountainous regions of Britain where they nest. These mid-May Dunlins passing through the estuary were heading further north. The lateness of the season certainly suggested that they were northern birds. Most of them had the black blazon on their underparts—their wedding dress—quite clearly defined, though a few were still showing indeterminate streaks. A rusty shade on their backs gave them a warm and comfortable look. They were very different from the sober, dun-coloured birds that gathered here two months ago.

A quarter of an hour passed and I was beginning to wonder whether any more visitors would grace the island with their presence today when, from over the shingle bank on the mainland, streamed an excited flock of noisy Oyster-Catchers. They alighted in the shallows quite near to the hide, a party forty strong, and, as they always do, they filled the air with strident clamour, conversing with each other at the tops of their voices before settling down to rest. Most of them were in full summer dress, but, surprisingly enough, there were half a dozen birds which still retained the necklet of white that is the distinguishing feature of their winter plumage. The resident population of breeding birds in this estuary rarely exceeds four pairs, so the great majority of these were migrants heading north. But whither were they bound? All over Britain the resident birds were settling in their breeding-haunts a month ago. Possibly these laggards were non-breeding birds shifting uneasily from coast to coast, unsettled by the seasonal change but lacking the fixity of purpose which dominates the great majority of adult birds when the reproductive urge takes hold of them.

Above the clamour of the Oyster-Catchers, suddenly, loud and clear, came the ' titti...titti...titti...' call of an approaching Whimbrel. This was a bird I was particularly hoping to see today, for May is the great month for migrant Whimbrel. Would it come in to alight with the other birds? I had my camera trained in readiness on the Oyster-Catchers and my eye glued to the focusing screen. Without any hesitation, down he came, and within a split second of alighting his image was recorded. In the next few moments I took four photographs of him in quick succession, for I could see that he was regarding the shingle mound uneasily and was liable to go at any moment. My suspicions were confirmed half a minute later, when he took to the air and joined some companions who flew over, headcalling invitingly as they went on their way.

54

A Whimbrel pays a fleeting visit

The tide was now narrowing the size of the island, and in the general confusion that attends the flooding of the estuary, birds were constantly on the wing and dropping in for fleeting visits. Four Grey Plovers alighted fifty yards away—an impossible distance even for a $24\frac{1}{2}$-inch lens—but they would not yield to the persuasion of the tide. They were all wariness, and it was tantalising to watch them at that distance and to note how three were still in partial summer dress and the fourth magnificently spangled in glorious black and silver. A party of five Knots soon came to join them, two of them startlingly ruddy of plumage and the others still clad in Quaker grey. When the water became too deep for them they swam a little nearer, but when the Grey Plovers decided it was time to go, the Knots went with them. In a few moments they were winging their way up the estuary and out of sight.

The Oyster-Catchers were now moving through the shallow water in single file, a sedate and suspicious procession, towards the spit of shingle where the Ringed Plover, with the water almost lapping up to the edge of her nest, was calmly brooding her eggs. Behind her, the nearest only a couple of feet away, were Dunlins, Turnstones and Oyster-Catchers, most of them by now far too somnolent to pay any attention to her precarious situation. But not all were sleeping. On the fringe of the group was a pair of Oyster-Catchers so absorbed in each other's charms that they had no time for relaxation. The nesting urge was strong upon them. One was busy turning round and

May—and one Oyster-Catcher still in winter plumage

round in the loose shingle busily excavating a nesting ' scrape,' whilst the other, with excited pipings, was patrolling to and fro as though applauding the whole performance. Here was a scene of strange contrasts—the tired migrants dozing away the high-tide hour, the Oyster-Catchers preoccupied with courtship, the Ringed Plover anxiously brooding her eggs—a scene such as only the month of May could give to one who would share with them the intimacy of the high-tide hour.

In the shallows within a few yards of the hide a score of Little Terns were bathing and preening, and, where space allowed on the shingles, they were making ' scrapes ' and calling to each other in the excitement of courtship. Occasionally a newcomer alighted with a silvery fish gleaming in its bill, and, waddling forward a few steps, it presented this token of regard with elaborate courtesy to a sitting bird.

Where the shingle bank sloped down to the water's edge a few Ringed Plovers were mingling with the sleeping Dunlins. Half-hidden in their midst was a smaller bird with unfamiliar plumage. The dark gorget on its breast was cleanly divided in the middle into two separate patches of dusky brown with white showing right up to the throat between them. There could be no doubt about it—it was a Kentish Plover. What strange chance had brought this bird, now practically extinct as a breeding species in the British Isles, to

56

A Kentish Plover appears amongst the somnolent Dunlins

to this little island today? The coincidence of its arrival here on the day I had chosen to acquaint myself with the estuary visitors in May lent a final touch to a wholly satisfying scene.

Here, on this narrow spit of shingle, with nesting and migration overlapping in this way, one could appreciate, as at no other time, the complex factors that underlie the movements and activities of the wader tribes.

One thing was abundantly clear—in different ways and at different stages, the same compelling purpose, the urge to reproduce their kind, had brought these birds together on this island at this time. The Ringed Plover quietly brooding her eggs in their midst was a bird nearing the fulfilment of that same purpose. The pair of Oyster-Catchers so deeply preoccupied with courtship were entering an earlier phase. But the migrants, some of them with still a thousand miles or more to fly before their breeding could begin, had not yet reached the courtship stage. Migration on this vast scale demands an expenditure of physical energy that allows little surplus for dalliance on the way. For them the first stirring of the reproductive urge had but one significance as yet—the summons of the north. And what of that chance visitor, the Kentish Plover? Whence had it journeyed, and whither was it bound? Was it a migrant pursuing a somewhat circuitous course to the Baltic regions, or was it a confused and solitary bird which had strayed from its normal haunts and been lost on passage? Or was it a survivor from that little colony on the Kentish coast which many think is now no more? Another possibility remained. Perhaps its unexpected presence here might indicate a westward colonising trend. Was it, in fact, a migrant, a straggler or a pioneer?

There is no end to the questions that are raised and the problems that are posed by a few hours in the estuary. No two visits are quite alike, and no one can predict what visitors may chance to come with wind and weather varying from day to day. But therein lies half its charm, for you never know what may turn up with the tide, and you come to share not only the secrets of the daily ebb and flow, but through the transitory visits of these feathered wanderers something, too, of the mysteries of that greater cycle of life in which all are bound. One factor, and one alone, is constant—the rising tide. Before it everything must yield. Gently insistent, it floods the waders' feeding-grounds. Before its irresistible advance they must retreat. To them the high-tide hours bring temporary loss: to one who would observe them at such times these precious hours are rich in opportunity, and I, for one, owe many of the happiest hours of my life to the kindly persuasiveness of tidal water.

7

The Godwits

OUT on the grey expanse of the estuary a few shore-birds are probing the tidal ooze. Diminutive Dunlins briskly quarter the muddy waste; Redshanks are working systematically through the shallow pools; here and there a Ringed Plover makes a rapid run and a sudden halt as it spies a toothsome morsel. A little further away the eye suddenly catches sight of a small group of larger waders with impressively long bills. Through the glasses, even though they are half a mile away, their identity is beyond question. They are Godwits—but are they Bar-Tailed or Black-Tailed Godwits? Only when the birds are flying can the tail-pattern be clearly seen. One must look for other features. They stand with a fine upright carriage, but they are not strikingly long-legged. Their bills are long and straight, but there is just a suggestion of an upward tilt to them. In the light of a late autumn afternoon their plumage appears to be a mottled brownish-grey; it is not noticeably dark as one had hoped. Almost certainly they are 'Bar-Tails,' but we must wait until the oncoming tide puts them to flight before we can be quite certain. In a few minutes up they go, and in so doing they put the matter of their identity beyond dispute. There is no white wing-bar, no broad black band on a white tail, and their feet project but slightly beyond the tail-feathers. With a feeling of slight disappointment we watch them depart, for it was the rarer Black-Tailed Godwit that we were hoping to see—which is really rather foolish, for a Godwit, whatever markings he carries on his tail, is always a bird to watch with great satisfaction, and one should never allow a desire for the unusual to dim one's appreciation of the commoner species. " Infatuation with the rare is the mark of a limited understanding," as a wise observer once remarked, and this is particularly true with the wader fraternity out in the estuary.

In suitable localities Bar-Tailed Godwits are very dependable waders, and there are few months in the year when they cannot be encountered. May is the month in which to see them in the full splendour of their breeding-plumage, when the rufous tinge that flushes the feathers of so many waders at this season envelops the male Godwits and suffuses a warmth to their dress which is in startling contrast to the soberness of their winter garb. On their northward journey, towards the middle of the month, they pass along our

Bar-Tailed Godwits, Oyster-Catchers and Grey Plovers—a typical group on an October day

coasts with such regularity that Norfolk fowlers have named the twelfth of May 'Godwit Day.' "Years ago the arrival of 'May Birds,' as these Godwits were called, used to be anxiously looked for by all the shore gunners round our southern and eastern coasts. On their first appearance they were generally exhausted by their long flight, and fell easy victims to their numerous assailants. If all the yarns of the Breydon wildfowlers are to be believed, these birds must in days gone by have visited the mud flats in that district in countless thousands. At the present day their numbers have sadly fallen off." So wrote E. T. Booth at the end of last century. As one of their 'numerous assailants,' he seemed reluctant to trace a connection between the wholesale massacre of the birds and a falling-off in their numbers; but that the two things went hand in hand is obvious, especially when we consider that the same reception greeted them on the return journey from their arctic breeding-grounds, when, as the same writer naïvely remarks: " Like the greater part of the birds that are reared in those deserted regions, they are of the most confiding disposition, appearing, unfortunately for themselves, to be totally unacquainted with the destructive propensities of man."

They arrive in the high north at the end of May, sometimes before the grip of the arctic winter has loosened. "The Samoyedes call the bird 'Tufek.' They said that she arrived very early in the spring, and ran round the frozen pools, tapping the ice with her long bill and crying impatiently for the thaw " (Seebohm). Out in the tundra, in a depression in the reindeer moss only recently exposed by the melting snow, the four eggs are laid. " One bird sits very close, while the other meets the intruder at least a mile from the nest, and never leaves him till he is clear of the neighbourhood, keeping up an incessant screaming, both when standing on the ground and when flying around " (Popham).

By the middle of July the young are already strong on the wing, and the southward passage begins. By the end of the month Bar-Tailed Godwits—mostly adults—are again in our estuaries. The young appear in strength with belated parents in August and September, and the southward passage to the Mediterranean and African coasts continues until October. After that month our winter residents, in varying numbers, are to be found on mud-flats around the coast, particularly in the southern half of the country. When you watch them out on the tidal ooze, plunging their bills nostril-deep in the succulent mud, or probing about in the shallows, you realise that you are looking at waders in their perfect setting: or see them on the wing, when for sheer zest of flying they will join forces with a company of Grey Plovers or smaller waders, following every twist and turn of those astonishingly intricate manœuvres, and you no longer wonder at the distances they travel when they obey the summons of the north and span half the globe to reach their breeding-grounds.

On more than one occasion I have had a Bar-Tailed Godwit's image on my focusing-screen during the high-tide hours, and whenever it has occurred I have experienced a feeling of great exhilaration. The Godwit is worthy quarry for the estuary photographer, and a single portrait of him is ample reward for many hours of waiting.

One day in the not too-distant future I hope to include the Black-Tailed Godwit's photograph in my portrait gallery. Half a century ago that would have been a very remote possibility indeed. But it is a curious thing that today, in spite of the intensive reclamation of coastal marshes and fen lands, and in spite of the ruination of so much of our coastline with pleasure resorts and bungalow towns, we stand a far better chance of seeing the Black-Tailed Godwit than did our grandfathers two generations ago. On the principle of " What is hit is history: what is missed is mystery " their sparse records of Godwits were generally of birds that had fallen victims to the guns of those who were possessed with the prevailing passion for skins. Today most of us go to the estuary armed only with binoculars and camera. We are content with sight records, and the Godwits live to give pleasure to others after our eyes have had their fill of them. But even so I do not believe that the decrease of persecution by gunners altogether accounts for the changed status of the Black-Tailed Godwit in this country. Fifty years ago it was a memorable day if a single bird was sighted. Today, especially from August to early October, it is not unusual to see small parties in a favoured estuary anywhere on the South Coast from Kent to Devon, though Chichester Harbour is probably the most favoured place of all. In one particular locality seven

Black-Tailed Godwit approaching nest

hundred or more of these magnificent birds can be seen flying in mass formation to the grassy meadows they use as high-tide roosts. The reasons for this marked increase in numbers are obscure. It is probable that we are witnessing a westward trend in the species comparable with the recent invasion of the country by the Black Redstart and the Little Ringed Plover.

In the muddy creeks that they frequent in preference to the open shore, their taller stature contrasts with the stockier 'Bar-Tails' should the two be seen together. Both are splendidly aristocratic, but the Black-Tailed Godwit is a prince amongst waders. Its plumage has an altogether darker hue, and once on the wing there can be no confusion. The broad, white wing-bar and the black band at the end of the gleaming white tail are very conspicuous: the legs, too, project well beyond the tail.

As a breeding-species the Black-Tailed Godwit, in contrast to the northern-nesting ' Bar-Tail,' frequents grassy meadows and marshland in countries which are, generally speaking, south of the Baltic. Before the reclamation of the fens it nested commonly in suitable localities in Great Britain, but, together with the Ruff and the Avocet, it departed from us a century or more ago. But, like the Avocet, it has shown, quite recently, considerable enterprise in attempting to re-colonise one or two of its former breeding-haunts. After the lapse of a century, a Lincolnshire fen has resounded again to the wild ' grütto...grütto...grütto' of a male Godwit rolling and twisting through the air in its majestic display-flight. But unlike the Avocet, with its specialised habitat which affords opportunity for intensive protection, the Black-Tailed Godwit does not stand a very good chance of becoming properly re-established. The Lincolnshire fen where, in 1940 and 1941, a pair successfully settled and bred, has now been drained so efficiently that potatoes are being grown where lush marsh grass formerly provided just the cover that the birds require. I visited this marsh in the last week of April, 1942, in the hope that these distinguished visitors might again be there, and I was not disappointed—but they were, for conditions had changed. A powerful draining-pump had been installed at the head of the ' Wash.' The dyke levels were appreciably lower, and the marsh grass was scrubby and parched. For an hour I watched the Godwits feeding and preening, and then, disturbed by a churlish pair of Carrion Crows, they took to the air, and, mounting to a great height, they made off in a north-easterly direction. To what green marsh that flight would take them I know not—possibly they were heading for the Dutch polders—their nearest breeding-grounds. Thither we must go today if we wish to interview the Black-Tailed Godwit at its nest. The accompanying photograph—very typical of the bird and its surroundings—was taken there by Grahame des Forges in the island sanctuary of Texel in 1945.

8

Curlew and Whimbrel

I HAVE always found the Curlew, that giant amongst the shore-birds, a most wary and sensitive creature. A camera lens, even at fifty yards, seems to have a most disconcerting effect on him; and the sacking hide, which so many waders ignore, is regarded by him with the utmost suspicion. And yet, if I wander on the green marsh with a dog for company, Curlews will throw caution to the winds and come whiffling down to mob my innocent

Curlews and Oyster-Catchers in the estuary

companion, showing a disregard for danger that is strangely inconsistent in so wary a creature.

At least there is no mistaking the Curlew, for no other wader has five inches of down-curved bill attached to a two-foot-long body. He stands on the shore, head, shoulders and upper parts above all the other waders, and he dwarfs them all. The Whimbrel, the only other bird with which there could be any possibility of confusion, is a mere two-thirds his size, with a bill not only two inches shorter, but less majestically down-curved. Should identity still be uncertain, the Whimbrel's crown with its contrasting streaks of light and dark can soon put all doubts at rest. And the cries of these two birds! What nostalgia is invoked in the city-dweller, what memories of wild and desolate places, when he hears those haunting calls raining down through the quiet skies at migration times; calls that are heard above the murmur that comes from great cities even in the hours of darkness—the Curlew's mournful repetition of its name, and the tittering note of the Whimbrel.

Out on the mud-flats the Curlew feeds in a manner deliberate and sedate, probing with his scimitar bill and ever-watchful of his neighbours. Inland a certain briskness is assumed when the food is of a more lively character, for beetles, earwigs and woodlice are snatched up greedily from the stubble fields

Stanton Whitaker

Curlew about to brood

and meadows to which the birds resort when the rising tide drives them from the slob-lands.

That a bird so elegant should have its digestive processes made the subject of an official enquiry is symptomatic of the trend of ornithology today. The trouble with the Curlew is that he cannot keep his gastronomic secrets to himself. He must, perforce, display his crop contents for an inquisitive world to inspect. On the rocks and grassy slopes of the remote and sea-girt islets to which he retires, full-fed, to digest his meals, he leaves behind him evidence of the past day's fare. Pellets, not unlike those that are ejected by Little Owls, are disgorged and scattered on the rocks. The eager ornithologist can reap a rich, if somewhat murky, harvest from a visit to these

Whimbrel at nest

T. M. Fowler

haunts, and let it not surprise him if he discovers in this romantic spot some curious little yellow pouches lying there. They are not, be it known, purses of elfin gold. They are the Curlews' gizzard linings. For reasons best known to themselves, these versatile birds renew their digestive apparatus from time to time, an operation which, after all, has much to commend it.

Today, through the medium of the radio, the Curlew's bubbling spring song is a familiar sound to millions who have never heard its haunting beauty in a natural setting. But every year the opportunity of hearing the song in unrecorded form is growing, for the Curlew's breeding range is steadily increasing, and there are river valleys and water meadows today in the Cheshire Plain and in the Severn and Trent valleys—to name but a few localities—where the birds are establishing themselves in ever-increasing numbers. The English countryside, abounding, as it does, with warblers and hedgerow birds, yet sadly lacks the impressive grandeur of the larger species. The lordly Curlew is a most welcome addition to any locality.

Whilst the Curlew continues to increase its range, the Whimbrel, for causes

66

Whimbrel and Oyster-Catchers, showing how nearly they approximate in size

unknown, appears to be on the retreat. A bird more at home in the sub-arctic regions, its breeding-haunts in Britain are restricted to the most northern parts of Scotland and to the outer islands. Like the Bar-Tailed Godwits that visit us with such regularity on passage to and from their breeding-grounds, Whimbrels are as predictable in their appearance as any bird could be. With the 'Bar-Tails' they share, amongst the fowling fraternity, the sobriquet of 'May Birds,' and there are few estuaries along our coast that do not give harbourage to these 'Half-Curlews' at their appointed seasons. No one could call the Whimbrel a confiding bird, but at least it does not take to the air with a distrustful backward glance when you are half a mile away, as happens so often with the Curlew. Indeed, there are times when you can watch a Whimbrel without the aid of glasses, and note his shorter, less decurved bill, and the distinctive pattern of his head-stripes. Once you have heard the 'titti...titti...titti...tit' cry you have his identity fixed for all time, and you think of him no longer as a Whimbrel, but, as the marshmen call him, a 'Titterel.'

I have occasionally had him within photographic range in the estuary at high tide when he will resort with Godwits and Oysters-Catchers to an island roost, but on the one occasion when I had him really close for any length of time, he insisted on dozing, one-legged, in an attitude that belied his natural grace of carriage; and to add to my despair he compelled me to photograph him with the sun shining straight into my lens. This was in August on the return migration, when most waders are more tractable than at other seasons. In May a Whimbrel that alighted for a few moments was all wariness. I doubt if he stayed for more than half a minute—just long enough for me to snatch an exposure or two before he took to the air, but I can still hear that wild call of his, melodious and far-reaching, with all the sweetness of spring in it, as he sped excitedly after others of his kind that were winging over the estuary towards the north. The Whimbrel is a bird that deserves well of the shore-photographer. One would like to do full justice to that finely streaked plumage of his, and to that down-curved bill that makes him so like and yet so distinct from the Curlew. Perhaps one day when I am hidden away in the estuary the two birds will alight side by side . . . perhaps!

9

The Woodcock

THE Woodcock is said to possess, for its size, one of the largest brains to be found in the bird world. It certainly needs every bit of it if the remarkable feats with which it is credited are to be performed. As happens with many crepuscular creatures, the witchery of twilight has invested the Woodcock with an aura of mystery and legend. It is well to remember that the Nightjar, another bird of the evening shadows, still bears the evil name of Goatsucker in many country places. With the Woodcock the legendary trend has taken a more complimentary turn, and the reason is not far to seek. As a table bird it has estimable qualities, and the hunter, whether primitive or civilised, is wont to praise before he slays.

As an instance of the intelligence the Woodcock is said to display may be mentioned the clever ruse which is adopted when the bird is seeking to deceive its prey, the humble earthworm. Tapping on the ground with its bill, and dancing up and down on widespread toes, the cunning bird can simulate the patter of falling rain. Deceived by the sound, the wretched worm comes streaking up to the surface, to be gobbled up with a knowing wink and a grunt of self-satisfaction by this exceeding wily bird. When damaged by shot, the Woodcock is furthermore credited with the ability to mend its own fractured limbs with a plaster of mud and feathers. In fact, nothing comes amiss to this enterprising bird.

But though stories of this kind may strain the credulity of the hearer, there is one feat which the Woodcock performs which has the stamp of authenticity upon it. No one any longer doubts its ability to transport its young ones by air from one place to another. There are countless accredited instances of this performance, and though there may be disagreement as to the actual method employed when the parent bird tucks the young under her body and becomes air-borne, the fact that she does so is no longer in dispute.

The status of the Woodcock in this country presents some interesting points. A hundred and fifty years ago it was a comparatively rare bird in the nesting-season, but at the beginning of the last century there were signs that a westward colonising movement had begun. Fifty years later a marked increase in nesting

R. Hallam

Woodcock approaching nest—a flashlight study

birds had taken place, and the western counties of England, and parts of Scotland and Ireland that had never before reported resident Woodcock, now had an increasing population. During the last half of the century the spread continued westwards, and Wales, the Lake District, and most of Scotland and Ireland were successfully colonised. In the present century the Isle of Man has been added to its conquests, but there has been a decrease in the southern counties of England and in the extreme north of Scotland.

Apart from this westward colonising trend that has been apparent for the last century and a half, there can be little doubt that the increase is due in the main to the cessation of the shooting of breeding birds in the nesting season, and to the protection of coverts in the interest of pheasant shooting. As we watch at dusk the lovely ' roding ' flights of Woodcock along the fringes of our plantations, we can reflect that here at least is one of nature's compensations to us for the loss to our countryside of the larger raptorial birds; for the increase of the one and the disappearance of the other are both by-products of the same idolatry. It is not the Woodcock but the Pheasant who is the real

'Cock o' the Woods.' I count amongst the happiest hours that I have had in quest of birds those that I have spent when searching for Woodcocks' nests in the early days of spring, when wind-flowers and primroses carpet the woodland glades, and shafts of sunlight come slanting through the trees, throwing a confusion of dappled light and shade on the dry, brown leaves that lie in drifts amongst the hazel thickets. It matters not how often the quest has been in vain, the setting has always been perfect. But should the searcher be rewarded, what a shock of pleasure awaits him when, amongst the russet leaves, his eye detects the still figure of a brooding bird, the marbled shadings of her plumage matching to perfection the surrounding leaves, a harmony of greys and browns that has no equal. Only the eye, that large and luminous eye, betrays the sitting bird, for unlike that other master of camouflage, the Nightjar, the Woodcock has not acquired the trick of narrowing her lids when brooding on her nest. It is as well for the searcher that she lacks this final touch.

In the woodlands of the south country which I know best, the Woodcocks nearly all depart, so the gamekeepers declare, on a full moon at the end of March. Very rarely a pair will stay to nest, but the majority of birds undoubtedly disappear with the coming of the Chiffchaff. When, in the hazel thickets, the tell-tale splashes of whitewash on the leaves and mosses are not renewed, we know that it is useless to search for Woodcocks' nests for another year. We shall not see Woodcock again until October. Then, one early autumn day on the sides of the Downs, from the shelter of a holly or juniper bush, a tired bird—and then another and another—will be flushed from under our feet, to rise stiffly and fly away reluctantly before pitching into cover at no great distance. They are weary, wing-stiffened birds newly arrived from the Continent, many from the Scandinavian or Baltic coast. Our resident Woodcock, like many resident waders, are sedentary in disposition and only disperse a short distance after the breeding season. Since colonising this country they have developed a stay-at-home disposition. They approve of our green and pleasant land, and I think that they deserve rather better treatment at our hands.

IO

Snipe

IF we disregard the extreme rarities—the lone American Snipe, for instance, that was recorded in the Outer Hebrides in 1920, and the twenty or more Red-Breasted Snipe (which, in any case, are not true Snipe) that have somehow found their way across the Atlantic and into our records—we are left with four different kinds of Snipe on the British list, and one of these, *Capella gallinago faeroeensis*, is a northern sub-species of the ordinary Common Snipe. It is found breeding in the Orkneys, Shetlands, Faeroes and in Iceland.

The Common Snipe, as resident, passage-migrant or winter visitor, is a familiar bird to the countryman, whose eyes are always gladdened when he see it rise from a boggy corner of a field with a hoarse 'scaap' and a bewildering zig-zag flight. It is familiar, too, to the city-dweller who sees its shot-riddled corpse hanging up in the poulterer's shop and may be excused for wondering why it should be hanging there at all.

The inland marsh in springtime would be incomplete without the 'drumming' of Snipe and the agitated 'chipper...chipper...chipper' of birds moving about in the tall marsh grass. All the year round and in all weathers Snipe are faithful to their chosen marshes, though numbers rise and fall with the periodic dispersal of breeding-birds and with the arrival of winter visitors from the Continent. Only when the ground is iron-hard in the grip of frost will they desert their boggy quarters. Under such conditions they are the first to suffer privation and hardship, for their long, sensitive bills cannot penetrate the frozen surface for the worms they must discover in order to keep alive. At such times they will resort to the sides of running streams or to muddy estuarine creeks, often in considerable numbers, where they can eke out a livelihood, though reduced by starvation and cold to a pitiable condition of tameness and apathy. There the man with a gun can seek them out, and he may, if he is so inclined, bag a dozen birds at a single shot, and boast about it afterwards in the local pub and display a haversack-full of pathetic bundles of feathers, skin and bone. Even the punt-gunner has been known to have a share in this shameful occupation, as witness the following record: " While punt-gunning one winter on a river in the north of Scotland, during a severe frost, I noticed

Common Snipe at nest—a typically moist situation

that Snipes were collected in numbers along the banks where the mud was kept soft by the action of the tide. As a novel proceeding I tried one shot at them with the big gun, but the poor birds were so tame that it could hardly be called sport" (E. T. Booth).

The status of the Snipe as a breeding species in this country has improved markedly during the last fifty years. At the beginning of the nineteenth century a decrease in the resident population was everywhere noted, the main cause being increasingly efficient draining of the land. This was followed by a steady dispersal and a subsequent increase, especially in southern England, where a breeding population, until then virtually non-existent, became established. In the early years of the present century a large area of the south Midlands was colonised, and many districts further west received their breeding-stock. There is no reason to suppose that this highly satisfactory state of affairs should not continue.

The Jack Snipe, which breeds in the marshes of northern Europe from the Arctic Circle to the southern shores of the Baltic, is, unlike many British waders, confined as a visitor to our country almost entirely to the late autumn and winter months. October, November and December are the best months in which to see Jack Snipe, though they continue to be seen until late March and April when passage birds are working through.

If, one late autumn day, you are crossing a belt of marshy ground and a solitary snipe of diminutive form rises reluctantly and silently from just under your feet, departing with comparatively slow wing-beats and with a fairly direct flight, only to pitch again into the marsh a short distance away, then the chances are that you have flushed a Jack Snipe. As likely as not it will give you another chance of flushing it and then you can look out for its distinctive features. It is noticeably smaller than the Common Snipe. Its bill is relatively shorter, and its streaked plumage has a metallic gloss. The crown feathers lack the Common Snipe's distinctive central stripe, and the tail feathers are uniformly dark, unrelieved by the white tips to the outer feathers which are quite noticeable in its larger cousin.

John Wolley was the first to describe the Jack Snipe's nesting-habits when, in 1853, he visited the great marsh of Muonioniska on the borders of Sweden and what is now Finland. His description of the occasion makes exciting reading nearly a century later: " At the time I could not at all guess what it was, an extraordinary sound unlike anything I had heard before. I could not tell from what direction it came, and it filled me with a curious suspense. My Finnish interpreter thought it was a Capercally and at the time I could not contradict him; but soon I found it was a small bird gliding at a wild pace at a great height over the marsh. I know not how better to describe the noise than by likening it to the cantering of a horse in the distance over a hard, hollow road: it came in fours, with a similar cadence and a like clear, yet hollow sound." It need hardly be added that Wolley eventually identified the bird as the Jack Snipe and succeeded in finding several nests, thus filling in another blank page in the history of waders. Later observers describe the song phonetically as 'Lok...toggi. Lok...toggi. Lok...toggi. Lok...toggi,' and the resemblance to Wolley's cantering horse is at once apparent. It should be put on record that Ralph Chislett found and photographed the Jack Snipe at nest in Lapland in 1926.

The Great Snipe, the last of our Snipes to be considered, is definitely a rarity. It is listed as ' a very scarce passage-migrant '—which means that though a few birds probably pass through eastern and southern England every year, the chances of seeing one of them is very remote, and should certainly be reported for inclusion in county bird records. It is considerably larger than the Common Snipe, larger in the wing and with a much heavier flight. It has a generally darker appearance than our other Snipes, but this darker hue is set off by a conspicuous amount of white on the sides of the tail.

74

Curiously enough the chances of seeing this rare visitor in marshland are not as great as on more elevated situations. It has a preference when on migration for rough hill pastures or bracken-covered slopes, though it is not averse to seeking shelter in sand-dunes when working down the coast. It is a bird of the middle Palæarctic region—that is, it nests in Norway, Sweden, Finland and parts of Russia.

A unique opportunity awaits the bird photographer who, armed with flashlight apparatus, could secrete himself at one of their display-grounds in the marshes and wait for nightfall and the arrival of Great Snipe who come to indulge there in the most fantastic communal courtship rites. Much of the display is vocal, and if the difficulties could be overcome the recording in sound of the Great Snipe's midnight symphony would be a unique achievement, and I have no doubt that Dr. Ludwig Koch has contemplated the project. R. Collet's description of the occasion is enough to excite the interest of anyone who is at all susceptible to the charms of these wading birds: " As soon as dusk commences to set in, and whilst it is still tolerably light, the ' Spil ' begins, and is continued throughout the night until early morning. The male bird utters a soft, almost warbling note, which is accompanied by a peculiar snapping sound caused by striking the mandibles together several times in quick succession. He then runs about the grass in front of the females, jumps every now and then on a tussock, puffs out his feathers and drops his wings. If a person approaches one of these drumming places he can hear at some distance the low note: ' bip-bip-bip-pip-bibipipere-bipere '; and then, within about a hundred paces, if the night is still, hear other sounds, which sometimes remind him of the distant cry of the Common Sandpiper, and sometimes of that of the Redshank, and intermingled with these a peculiar hissing or piping note which seems almost incomprehensible."

With the approach of dawn the frenzy of excitement dies down, and the midnight revellers go their several ways in pairs to the hidden swamps where, in due course, their families will be reared. Out of the breeding-season the Great Snipe is the most silent of birds, emitting, at the most, a low grunt of protest when flushed. It would seem as if the pent-up emotions of a twelve-month are all released in those few hours of wild, ecstatic revelry and song.

II

The Phalaropes

PHALAROPE—a word that comes 'trippingly on the tongue,' romantic and intriguing— aname that summons up a vision of a seven-inch waderling riding the waves in mid-ocean as lightly as a paper boat, or spinning round on its axis in a shallow lagoon to stir up the animalcules that are lurking below the surface; or, if the mind's eye is directed northwards, one glimpses a vast migratory flight by oceanic routes to Polar regions, where, blue legs twinkling over the melting snow or threading their way through a forest of cotton grass, the Phalaropes conduct a curiously inverted courtship in which the quasi-reluctant male is harried and pursued, is displayed to and wooed, by an ardent female whose vigilance thereafter ensures that he, and he alone, shall brood the eggs until the next generation of the genus *Phalaropus* is safely swimming in an arctic loch.

So far can imagination take us. In point of fact, the name Phalarope means nothing more than ' Coot-footed '—a neat scientific label to describe the physical characteristic that distinguishes these pelagic waders from the rest of their kindred. In them the love of moist and muddy haunts, that has its origin far down the stem of the wader race, finds its ultimate expression. They have committed their fate to the ocean itself, and on its heaving surface they conduct their daily affairs, except when the call to reproduce their kind summons them to their marshy breeding-haunts, or when continuous storms at sea compel them to seek the shelter of some inhospitable coast, where their astonishing tameness—the result of a complete unfamiliarity with the predatory instincts of land animals and in particular of man—too often leads to their destruction.

We have two Phalaropes that grace the British list. The Grey Phalarope, a north Holarctic species that breeds in the arctic, and the Red-necked Phalarope, a bird that belongs truly to the northern islands of Sweden, Finland and Norway, but whose southern range just includes the Orkneys, Shetland and the Outer Hebrides, where its status as a breeding bird, owing to the depredations of collectors, was rendered precarious indeed until fairly recent times, when, through protection, it has made a partial recovery. A small outlying colony also exists on a privileged corner of the Irish coastline in co. Mayo.

Red-Necked Phalarope in winter plumage   *F. P. J. Kooymans*

Unless we have the good fortune to visit one of these breeding-haunts, our chances of encountering a Phalarope are not very great. The Red-necked is an unusual passage-migrant, and both species are only exceptionally seen inland. The Grey, though occurring more frequently along the coast, is only seen in any numbers after continuous gales in September and October. Just as there are good Waxwing and Crossbill years, so there are good Grey Phalarope years. The most recent irruption occurred in October and November (an unusually late month) in 1934. Several exceptional invasions occurred in the latter half of last century, and an account of Grey Phalaropes on the Sussex coast at that time sets one wondering what one autumn day may hold in store should the same stormy conditions be repeated this year—or next. " After unusually severe gales in September and October they are occasionally found in immense numbers. Should the storm continue many days they seem to suffer greatly from its effects, and scores may be seen so exhausted that they allow themselves to be caught by hand. In the middle of September 1870 I observed a few passing along the south coast, and after a heavy south-east gale about three weeks later, hundreds were found in the neighbourhood of Brighton, and the flight extended as far west as Plymouth. I picked up nearly a dozen one morning, so disabled by the storm and by want of food as to be incapable of flying; numbers at the same time being seen hovering

77

over the breakers a short distance at sea. They kept passing for nearly a fort-night, a few being noted on fine days, but several shewing themselves in small pools near the sea-beach in rough or windy weather " (E. T. Booth).

We never know what a blustery autumn day may hold in store, and it is well to know what may turn up under conditions that might well tempt the fine-weather bird watcher to stay by the fireside.

Should a Phalarope come under observation there are certain character-istic features that should be noted if one is to distinguish the Red-necked from the Grey—by no means a simple thing to do when both birds are in winter plumage from which the rufous tints of their breeding-dress have disappeared. Both are now mantled in grey and white, but the back of the Red-necked Phalarope is a darker grey in tone than its relative, and there are whitish streaks which give it a less uniform appearance. The wings are darker, too, with a more prominent white wing-bar. It sits higher in the water and appears to swim with a greater buoyancy. But the chief distinguishing feature is the bill. The Red-necked Phalarope has a noticeably longer and more slender bill. The Grey Phalarope's bill is not only shorter and broader, but it is decidedly yellow in hue, and it has a black tip.

In summer dress there can be no confusion. The Grey has chestnut underparts and whitish sides to its face, and its back is a handsome dark brown streaked with chestnut. The Red-necked Phalarope, with a lovely orange patch on the sides of its neck, slate-grey head and upper parts, white throat and underparts, is unique.

12

The Knot

Hamlet. Do you see yonder cloud that's almost in shape of a camel?
Polonius. By the mass, and 'tis like a camel, indeed.
Hamlet. Methinks it is like a weasel.
Polonius. It is backed like a weasel.
Hamlet. Or like a whale.
Polonius. Very like a whale.

If Shakespeare had made this conversation take place on the mud-flats of the Kattegat instead of in the castle at Elsinore it would no longer be a pleasant piece of fooling but a curiously appropriate description of one of the most amazing spectacles that await the bird-watcher in any of the great estuaries of the European coastline. The separate particles of that ever-changing cloud are not drops of condensed vapour but living birds, thousands and thousands of living birds, flying in a formation so dense that the sky is darkened as they pass. When Knots are on the move they travel in nations, and their numbers defy all attempts at computation. " A nation of Knots speeding over the sea approaches the land like a grey rain-cloud, constantly altering its shape and shifting its altitude as the birds pursue their intricate mazes through the air. . . . As the corporate legion draws nearer, the roar of its multitudinous wings is like the booming of high waves at the foot of limestone caverns " (H. J. Massingham).

At feeding-time as they spread out in a grey carpet over the mud, they show the same orderliness in their movements as they do when in the air, for they move steadily forward in the same direction, and, like as not, will suddenly take to the air to perform some astonishing evolution before streaming down to the same spot that they were occupying before. In dress, as we see them in the winter, Knots are soberly apparelled in Quaker grey, and they have eyes like black buttons. Their build is stocky and their manner of feeding is fussy. Considerably larger than the Dunlins who will invariably be seen in the vicinity, Knots more nearly approach the size of Redshanks, though appearing very squat and short of stature when standing in their company, as they quite like to do at a high-tide roost. In the late spring, when the northward passage starts to breeding-grounds in the Arctic that are so remote that few

A Knot and a Dunlin in the shallows

have ever seen the nest of this elusive wader, we may see Knots whose under-parts are suffused with cinnamon, and a few birds on the return migration in August and September still bear the same vivid hue which has earned for the American race the name of 'Redbreast' or 'Beach Robin.'

The Knot is a bird which still keeps many of its secrets to itself. Nestlings were discovered by the Nares Polar Expedition in Grinnell Land in 1876, but the first authenticated eggs were not taken until the turn of the century, when Dr. Walter obtained them on the Taimyr Peninsula in 1901. Even now, nearly fifty years later, all that we can say is that the Knot is known to breed in northernmost Siberia, Spitzbergen, Greenland and some Canadian arctic islands. Somewhere in a northern region as yet unexplored there must be a vast breeding-ground to which resort the millions of birds that every winter spread around the shores of the world.

In former days the flesh of the Knot was much esteemed, and great slaughter was executed amongst the flocks that were working south after the breeding-season. " The young on their first arrival in the autumn occasionally suffer themselves to be shot at time after time without making the slightest attempt to escape, the survivors of the flock simply rising on wing at each discharge, and after a short flight settling again with the dead and wounded " (E. T. Booth). They were also netted by the wildfowlers and fattened for the table in the same manner as Ruffs, a practice that was carried on three centuries ago, as we know from the writings of Sir Thomas Browne: " Gnats or

The vanguard of a flock of Knots hurtling past the hide

Knots, a small bird which taken with netts grow excessively fat. If being mewed and fed with corne, a lighted candle in the roome, they feed day and night, and when they are at their hight of fattnesse they beginne to grow lame and are then killed.''

The American species of Knot used to be taken out on the mud flats at night by a crude method known as ' Fire-lighting.' Two men would start out after dark at half-tide, one of them carrying a lighted lantern, and the other a bag which he kept slung over his shoulder. When near a flock of Knots, they would approach them on their hands and knees, and the man with free hands would reach out cautiously and seize the birds one by one, bite their necks, and slip them into his bag. Hundreds of birds were taken in a single night, and after a few years of this intensive slaughter the numbers of Knots began to show such a marked decrease that the practice was made illegal. It would be interesting to try this method of stalking them today, with a view to taking flashlight photographs of the sleeping flocks. At least no harm would come to the birds, and even if no photographs resulted one would not be returning with a bagful of corpses, a guilty conscience and a nasty taste in one's mouth.

13

The Turnstone

THE Turnstone deserves a chapter to himself, not only because he does not fit in easily into any of the other wader groups, but because he is, of all the small shore-birds, an individualist in appearance and in disposition. Most of the waders are dainty feeders, probing for their food with sensitive bills, or snatching up their elusive prey with a deft movement of those beautifully delicate forceps with which they are endowed. The Turnstone has discovered another method of approach. He heaves and shoves his way along the tide-line, levering away at stones with his miniature pick-axe bill, or thrusting his head in a purposeful manner amongst the tangles of seaweed; and the harvest of sand-hoppers and maggots that he discovers in this way is proof, if any were needed, that there is a rich reward for anyone in this world who has a really original idea and is prepared to exploit it. Once the Turnstone's stocky, determined little figure has been detected on the rock-strewn shore—and it is by no means easy to pick out nine inches of mottled wader against this background—you have his identity assured. Though he will stray out on to the flats, his true habitat is the high-tide line, especially if there are rocks and seaweed to be explored there, and his companion in these haunts is the Purple Sandpiper, who shows such a marked preference for his company that it is difficult to believe that there is not a business understanding between the two species.

T. A. Coward remarked of Turnstones, " Happy the man that first names them Tortoiseshell Plovers." It is a very apt description of the bird, especially if one's first glimpse of him is when he is in full breeding-dress, for 'tortoiseshell' and chestnut are the predominant colours of the upper parts, and a chequering of black and white on the head and throat, and a broad dark band on the chest which contrasts handsomely with clear white underparts, give to the Turnstone a striking appearance which it retains, though considerably subdued and toned-down in the winter months, so that at all seasons he has something of the harlequin in his appearance. In flight the pattern is strikingly pied, and an oval patch of white on the rump stands out clearly when the bird is in the air. Vivid orange legs add a final touch of the

Turnstones in August in full breeding-plumage and partial moult. A Redshank has strayed into their midst

bizarre to his colourful appearance. The call-note, a metallic 'kitititit,' is very striking.

Not all the Turnstone's food is obtained by bulldozing methods. He has a penchant for small edible mussels, and will attack them in a manner identical with that adopted by the Oyster-Catcher, piercing mussel shells through the dorsal and ventral borders or at the posterior end; but whereas the Oyster-Catcher chooses mussels up to two inches in length, the Turnstone recognises his limitations and is content with half-inch shells. Small limpets are dislodged from the rocks with a sudden jab, or are even levered off by sheer muscular strength, and their contents devoured. The American forms of Turnstone, races only geographically different from ours, have been observed indulging in a form of depravity which, I am glad to say, has not been reported in our own species. On their northward passage, which they delay until many other birds are already nesting, they have been seen working systematically through a colony of nesting Terns, smashing and sucking the eggs as they went. Perhaps it is as well that our Terns are not generally nesting until the northward passage of waders is almost completed. Though a few Turnstones are to be seen in full breeding-plumage throughout the summer, especially in the

Turnstones in March. An argument between birds in winter plumage

north of Scotland and in the outer islands, the bird has never yet been proved to breed in this country. Its most southerly haunts are islands in the Baltic, though the majority of birds go much further north and breed in west Greenland, Iceland, Spitzbergen and on the northern coastline of Europe. It has a great love for islands, where its eggs are laid in a scantily lined hollow amongst the boulders or sparse vegetation.

This preference for islands marks the Turnstone's behaviour not only in the breeding-season, but also during its stay in this country, and the estuary photographer can usually reckon on a few of these colourful birds consenting to share with him the high-tide hours. They show a marked liking for a lofty perch, and if a bank of shingle can be raised in a suitable place beforehand it will be sought out by Turnstones, who will obligingly stand within photographic range if all goes well. If compelled to share their perch with other waders, a certain irritability in their constitution breaks out, and a chorus of deep-throated growls surges through the company—a noise strangely reminiscent of that which swells out from time to time on overcrowded Guillemot ledges.

After high tide, during the hour of relaxation, Turnstones show complete abandon when they take their ease. They sprawl about and sun themselves, fluffing out their feathers, only breaking off occasionally to swear half-heartedly at a stranger who has strayed in their direction. An inquisitive bird may even come right up to the hide and start poking about questioningly amongst the boulders that are holding the canvas in place.

I have a great affection for Turnstones. Birds that show decidedly individual character, as they do, stand out from the rest. They seem to know what they want to do in this life, and they don't believe in doing things by halves.

14

Dunlin and Curlew-Sandpiper

I REGARD the Dunlin as a trusted friend. Other rarer and more elusive species may claim my attention by their transitory visits when I am concealed on an island sanctuary at high tide, but I know full well that they would not be there at all were it not for the confidence inspired in them by the presence of the more dependable waders, in the roll of which I accord the Dunlin the place of highest honour. And after the others have departed there are nearly always a handful of Dunlins that remain, their little bodies hunched up in perfect repose, and often enough I have tired first of the long wait imposed on us all by the slowly receding tide, and have had to emerge from my hiding-place and disturb their slumbers.

The commonest of all the shore waders, Dunlins are present on the mud-flats in every month of the year, though their numbers swell to prodigious proportions when the northward migration is in full swing in March and April, and when the southward passage is in progress during August and September.

In a stack-yard in winter one tends to assume that all the small birds foraging and twittering there are finches and sparrows. In the same way, unless there is a good reason for believing otherwise, one tends to assume that all the small waders busily dibbling out on the tidal ooze are Dunlins— which is really a tribute to this ubiquitous little wader, for it must have achieved a very satisfactorily balanced economy to be able to maintain its status and remain unquestionably the commonest and the most widely distributed of all the shore waders. Nor does it follow a stereotyped pattern either of behaviour or of physical proportions. It obtains its food in a variety of pleasing ways. It shows a catholicity of taste in its habitats that contrasts strongly with many of the more fastidious members of the wader tribe. It frequently occurs inland, and is a regular visitor to sewage farms. To assert that it is amongst the waders as the Starling is amongst passerine birds is not as uncomplimentary as it may sound, for the success of a species is best judged by its status in a changing world. Both birds have the same adaptability, the same disregard for conven-tion, the same mutually helpful social traits, and both are marked successes in an age that is witnessing the rapid decrease of many more specialised species. The Dunlin shows marked individuality in bodily size and in the length of its

Dunlins in August, most of them still in breeding-dress

bill. This independence of attitude is also shown in the remarkable disregard which it shows for doffing and donning its bridal attire—that characteristic black smudge on the breast which is its truly diagnostic feature—at the appropriate seasons. When all the other waders are in the full glory of their nuptial array a casual Dunlin may be seen trotting around the mud flats in his dowdy winter dress, rather like a guest who turns up at an evening dress affair in an open collar and corduroy trousers. Similarly, when all the other waders in October have donned their winter dress, a cheerful Dunlin will appear still wearing his black waistcoat. He just hasn't bothered to change.

But though one may poke fun at the Dunlin for his charming eccentricities, there is one sphere in which he displays supreme artistry. When he takes to the air with a myriad others of his kind there is no other bird that can sink his individuality so completely in producing a perfectly co-ordinated display of aerial gymnastics, as H. J. Massingham so aptly describes in a passage which, to me, conveys the very essence of what is a supremely artistic performance. " They will be pottering to and fro with twittering ejaculations when, all of a sudden, each separate note has flowed into a tune. The Dunlin

87   G

Dunlin approaching its nest on the moors

are in the air and all, as by an invisible broom, are swept into a perfect unison of movement. They change pattern, direction, colour and formation with every turn, but each individual keeps the same distance from his neighbours, the same momentum and the same angle of the body that they do, as though they were all pulled hither and thither from the ends of an infinite number of equidistant threads, held by an unseen hand—thousands of leaderless birds with the cohesion of one body, supported upon one pair of wings.

"The afternoon sun hurls long bright shafts athwart the silent marshes when suddenly one of these tremendous floods of life surges over them, rising and falling, banking and curving, and accompanied by a hiss of wings and a soft purr or humming from innumerable throats. Then, as though they swam into a magnetic spell, breathed from the brown flats beneath them, they stay their course, swerve at right angles with a concurrent tilt of bodies, flash a single sheet of white and sweep the air an inch above the ground in one precipitate wave. The marshland pulls them to its breast and they sink into it, breaking up at once into a jargoning scurry of individuals, confusedly twinkling over its surface."

The host of scurrying waders on the mud flats should be scrutinised with especial care in early autumn, in case one should overlook a Dunlin-like waderling with a longish bill that is slightly decurved—rather more noticeably so than is the case with the average long-billed Dunlin. The Curlew-Sandpiper, or Pigmy Curlew, is not an uncommon bird during the autumn passage, but it is uncommonly easy to overlook at this season, a mistake that one could not make in the spring when it has rufous underparts of an even brighter hue than the cinnamon-breasted Knot in breeding-plumage. Its flight, like its bill, is a curving one, or perhaps it is truer to say that it is a series of switchbacks reminiscent of a finch. But once in the air its startlingly white rump is at once visible, and no further clue is needed as a pointer to its identity. When standing amongst Dunlins it has a more slender carriage, a more upright stance and distinctly longer legs than its humdrum cousins. It is my hope every time that I visit the estuary to fill in a blank in my gallery of wader portraits with a photograph of the Curlew-Sandpiper, but so far it has eluded me. The only photograph that I have seen of this little wader on the mud flats in this country is a distant shot by my friend and fellow-enthusiast John Reynolds, but unfortunately it just misses being good enough for reproduction.

15

The Stints

MARSHMEN use the word Stint as a collective term which embraces all the small waders that flicker over the muddy wastes. The name correctly belongs to three birds on the British list, and one of these is an American straggler that has only been identified four times in the last hundred years, which leaves us with two Stints to watch for, one that is of regular though never plentiful appearance, the Little Stint, and the other of irregular occurrence and of considerable rarity, Temminck's Stint.

Stints are the most diminutive of all the waders, which can be shown by a comparison of their size with some of the more familiar passerine birds. If we take the Dunlin as a norm for the measurement of shore-birds (a somewhat variable norm, as Dunlin vary in size from $6\frac{3}{4}$ to $7\frac{1}{2}$ inches) we may say that a Dunlin approximates in size to a Song Thrush if an inch is docked off the latter's tail. The Little Stint is the same length as a Chaffinch, though plumper of body and shorter of tail. He is a full inch shorter than the Dunlin and an inch makes a lot of difference in a small waderling.

Calidris minuta is the Little Stint's textbook name, and to appreciate the significance of the word *minuta* the Little Stint should be seen, as I first saw him one October day, standing with his toes in shallow water and considering with grave demeanour the reflection of his tiny form in the mirror at his feet, with mile upon mile of shimmering sand and gleaming mud stretched out on every side of him. He stood quite still for a quarter of an hour, and allowed me to note at leisure every detail of his tiny form—the exquisite pale grey of his mantle, the dazzling purity of his underparts, and the set and poise of his short and straight and finely pointed bill. Eventually he flickered off with a clear ' chit-chit-chit.' A few weeks later and he would be past the Equator, heading for the Cape or the Indian Ocean, and then, with the return of spring, he would be speeding north again to the Arctic, where his breeding-grounds in Europe remained undiscovered until 1875, when Seebohm and Harvie-Brown found an outlying colony nesting on the swampy tundra near the mouth of the Petchora River. They found that nesting Stints were astonishingly tame, an observation later confirmed by Miss M. D. Haviland when she photographed the bird at nest near Golchika.

" I went to the place armed with a large reflex camera, racked out to its fullest extent. It seemed rather like taking a siege gun to shoot rabbits, but the bird was so small that I feared that she would not appear on the plate at all unless a lens of long focus was used. But it turned out to be quite unnecessary. The chief difficulty was to get far enough away from the sitter, who tripped round my feet not afraid, but just a little nervous lest I should

J. E. Sluiters

Little Stint—an immature bird in autumn plumage

accidentally crush her eggs. When I touched the nest she sprang up almost as if she would have flown at me, and then toddled sideways with wings trailing distractedly, and puffed-out feathers. The tameness of the Little Stint at the nest is quite uncanny. It seems as if the life of the race that she fosters has power for a season to raise the bird above such commonplace matters as food and fear, and fills her with a sort of ecstasy of maternity. Later on, when the eggs are chipping, this passion to brood rises to such a pitch that the bird will actually suffer itself to be taken in the hand rather than leave her nest. I use the words he and she indiscriminately when writing of the Stints, for both sexes share the duties of incubation." Trevor-Battye had a similar experience near Kolguev, and he describes an agitated Little Stint at the nest as behaving " like a dancing-doll, jumping up and down on the same spot as if on springs."

When seen in this country in the autumn—generally from mid-August to October—Little Stints appear singly or in small parties, and they frequent the same terrain as Dunlins. They are, in fact, in habits and appearance very like diminutive Dunlins.

The Temminck's Stint, on the other hand, is like a diminutive Sandpiper, preferring creeks and gutters to the open flats, and often resorting to fresh-water marshes. In size it is even smaller, by half an inch, than the Little Stint. Its general appearance is greyer, and its breast has not the same pearly whiteness. Furthermore, when it rises, it shoots straight up into the air like

Ralph Chislett

Temminck's Stint

a Snipe, and calls with a high-pitched trilling titter, quite different from the monosyllabic ' chit-chit-chit ' of the Little Stint.

Its breeding-range is not quite so northerly as the Little Stint's, and it made ornithological history in this country by nesting in the Cairngorm district in 1934 and 1936.

Miss M. D. Haviland described the display-flight of courting birds as one of the most charming things she had ever witnessed. " The bird took wing suddenly, and spun away down the river bank with a high, shrilling call: ' Trrrrrr.' Sometimes it sank down, tired out by the spring ecstasy, but more often it circled slowly round, head to wind, and hovered for a while with rapidly vibrating wings and throat. When a number of birds thus hung poised in the air the effect was very charming." Dan Meinertzhagen similarly described the performance as he saw it in northern Finland. " They fly about, when the sun is shining, exactly like a lark, hovering over a place and uttering a twittering note, which is apparently kept up the whole time they are on the wing. They are absurdly tame, sometimes flying by within a yard, and settling close to one. They look scarcely larger than the House Martins which fly over the same area." But Miss M. D. Haviland found that, unlike the Little Stint, they were timid nesters. A Temminck's Stint she tried to photograph was " . . . unusually shy, and at each exposure the click of the shutter drove her away with a flash of small dagger-grey wings. She never flew directly on to her eggs, but always alighted a little distance away and ran up in little zig-zag rushes between the willows. Her small grey body and jerky movements made her seem more like a mouse than a bird."

In this country, even if we have easy access to mud-flats and saltings, to fresh-water marshes and sewage farms, we shall be fortunate if we see a Temminck's Stint more than once or twice in a lifetime, but we need not, on that account, write off the Stints as impossible of acquaintance. Every autumn, and occasionally in the spring, Little Stints appear amongst our flocks of shore-birds, using our coastal marshes as a temporary refuge on their southward or northward journey. The larger waders may make a more impressive spectacle, but size is no criterion in the world of living things. Ben Jonson's reflections, though they may sound a little trite, still ring very true:

> " In small proportions we just beauties see:
> And in short measures life may perfect be."

16

The Sanderling

SANDERLINGS flock in to a high-tide roost in the late summer and early autumn in great strength, and there have been occasions when my hide has been entirely surrounded by them. They mingle to some extent with Dunlins, but even when the press of birds has reached its maximum density it is usual to see a certain orderliness in the groupings of the various species. Turnstones like to have plenty of elbow room, but Dunlins and Sanderlings will pack together tightly. Ringed Plovers just wander about anywhere, and get chivvied by the others for their restlessness. But satisfying though it is to have Sanderlings for company at the high-tide hour, I always feel that they are not really at home on the hard rocks or shingles. They are essentially birds of the water's edge, where the breakers ceaselessly pound the yellow sands. Sanderling is the bird's name, and sand—as opposed to mud—is its true habitat. I like to see my Sanderlings away at the edge of the tide. It matters not whether the tide be coming in or going out. It is all one to Sanderlings, and the bigger the waves the more zest is attached to the adventure of snatching up their food, as it were, in the very jaws of the friendly monster. If the beach shelves fairly steeply so that the waves rush for a few yards uphill and as rapidly retreat, a party of Sanderlings can afford as entertaining a half-hour as any that you are likely to have at the edge of the tide. Strung out in a long line, they pursue the receding wave, eagerly snatching up morsels as they go, until, just in the nick of time, they turn about and scamper furiously up the beach as the next breaker comes crashing down behind them. But no sooner has it spent its force than they are twinkling down the slope again, their little legs a-blur with the rapidity of their pursuit. And so it goes on by the hour.

When they tire of this pursuit you will find them dreaming away on the flats, etherial beings in the palest of grey mantles, with pearly-white underparts that catch the light and hold it in an extraordinary way, and should they be on wet sand each bird is attended by its own luminous reflection. They walk hand in hand with their own bright spirits.

In the air Sanderlings display a prominent white wing bar, and, like all the shore-waders, they indulge in social flights that have their own peculiar beauty. They have a way of swinging their bodies from side to side in perfect

94

Sanderlings mixing with Dunlins. An August photograph when most birds are still in partial breeding-dress

unison, so that at one moment you see a shimmer of white, and the next a pattern of grey, and there are times when they disappear from view entirely, only to reappear a moment later, a flash of silvery stars, as they heel over slantwise in another direction.

Many pass the entire winter here, though the majority travel far to the south of these islands. Any sandy cove around our shores is likely to produce a little flock even in the darkest days. With the return of spring the silver-grey on the back is replaced by light chestnut mottlings interspersed with black, but the breast remains as pearly as it ever was.

The Sanderling was one of the mystery birds to ornithologists of last century. The first authentic eggs were taken by Macfarlane near Franklin Bay in 1863, and the Nares Polar Expedition returned with a clutch of eggs from Grinnell Land in 1876. A. L. V. Manniche photographed a nesting bird in north-east Greenland in July, 1908, but even today remarkably few nests have been discovered. Like the Knot, it guards its secret haunts uncommonly well.

17

Ruff and Reeve

IT is a little ironical that one whose home is in Lincolnshire should be writing in praise of the Ruff, for it was in that county, and particularly in the town of Spalding, that the trade of fattening Ruffs, netted in the surrounding fens, was chiefly carried on, a practice which, with the increased efficiency in drainage, eventually led to the extermination of the species in this country. The curious may read a very complete account of this in the *Supplement* to Montagu's *Ornithological Dictionary*. An earlier account of the method of fattening these and other waders is to be found in *The Plain-dealing Poulterer* published in London in 1699: "Godwites, Knots, Roofes and Curlewes which are esteemed of all other the daintiest and dearest should be fed on fair Childer wheat and water, but if you wish to have them extra-ordinary and crammed, then you must take the finest drest Wheat-meal, and mixing it with milk, make it into a Paste, and as you knead it, sprinkle into it the grains of small Wheat till the Paste be fully mixt therewith; then make little small crams thereof, dipping them in water, give to every Fowl according to his bigness, till the gorge be well fill'd; do this as oft as you shall find the gorge empty."

It is pointless to censure our forefathers for attempting to provide fresh meat for the table at a time when most families would go for weeks in the winter and spring without tasting meat at all. The cattle ranges of the Argentine and the sheep farms of Australia and New Zealand have played quite a considerable part in altering our outlook on birds during the past century. But the demand for birds' flesh did not diminish in time to save the Ruff. By the middle of last century it was a dying race, and although it has made occasional efforts to breed here since, it seems improbable that it will ever re-establish itself in these islands again. When a species that requires the stimulus of social encounter as an integral part of its breeding-cycle is reduced below a certain point it tends to disappear. In any case, the intensive cultivation of the fens and the almost total disappearance of grassy inland marshes leaves it little room to breed even should it show an inclination to return to its old haunts.

To describe the Ruff's springtime attire as fantastic is to confess how little

Ruffs displaying on a 'tilting-ground' in the Dutch polders

we know of the inner significance of such adornment in the mating season, but when a wader that in winter plumage looks like a rather dowdy Redshank suddenly blossoms forth with a pair of lappets that may be black or white or purple or orange or any indeterminate shade between; lappets which it can raise until they give the owner a frill more impressive than that worn by the most exquisite of Elizabethan gallants—well, it does rather look as if nature has indulged in a little unnecessary extravagance. The significance of the Ruff's adornments is clearly linked up with its remarkable social behaviour. Space will not permit a detailed description of the communal display that occurs in the latter half of April on their 'leks' or 'tilting-grounds.' Suffice to say that Edmund Selous, that most wise and patient of field naturalists, who spent three weeks of continuous observation of these birds at a 'lek' in the spring of 1906, proved conclusively that the males do not fight for possession of the females as was previously believed. It is the females who do the choosing of their partners, and, for the most part, they move about serenely and composedly whilst the Ruffs indulge in a frenzy of contortions and crouchings and sparrings with their neighbours, all of a curiously formalised character, more appropriate to a charade or a masquerade than to a battle-ground.

In Britain we are most likely to see an occasional Ruff or Reeve on the autumn passage. By this time the Ruff's extravagant garb has been discarded, and both birds are similarly plumaged, though the males are considerably larger than the females. It is more often young birds that are seen in this country. But for its darker rump it closely resembles the Redshank at this season, but there is a gravity in its deportment and a stiffness in its gait that is noticeable. Also it is a remarkably silent bird, and when it flies, it speeds away with strong regular beats of its wings with an occasional glide in between. Its bill is rather shorter than a Redshank's, and so are its legs, which show almost as much variation of colour as do its lappets in springtime. In flight the central area of the tail is dark, but clear oval white patches show on either side. It also lacks the white secondaries that are so prominently shown by a Redshank on the wing.

If we wish to see the Ruff in its breeding-haunts today we must go to Holland, and I am indebted to F. P. J. Kooymans for permitting me to reproduce one of his remarkable photographs of these birds on their tilting-ground in the Dutch polders.

18

The Sandpipers

THE bird-watcher who turns his attention to the Sandpiper family may well be discouraged when he discovers that there are eighteen different species bearing the name Sandpiper in the British list. But for practical purposes it is not as difficult as it appears to be, for thirteen of these are extreme rarities, so rare in fact that I doubt if a single museum can claim to have a complete series of British-killed specimens of all the Sandpiper species. The five Sandpipers which a patient observer may justly hope to see in the course of his watchings are: Common, Green, Wood, Purple and Curlew-Sandpiper—though I hasten to add that the latter two species are not exactly true Sandpipers, but relatives of the Dunlin and Stint. For convenience they have been included here, but the fact is that, in common with five of the extreme rarities that bear the name Sandpiper, they really belong to different, though closely allied, families. Early ornithologists were wont to use the name Sandpiper as a convenient label for any unusual small wader that came their way, and it is difficult to discard time-honoured terminology, as those who seek to re-name the Hedge Sparrow have discovered.

It is as well to get to grips with the rarer species first, if only to slay the bogy of the unknown, and to convince ourselves that the elusive little wader we glimpsed in the creek the other day was not a Semi-Palmated Sandpiper after all. This particular species (a greyer form of the Little Stint with a suggestion of webbing between its toes) has strayed over from America and been recorded in this country precisely—once. The American Pectoral Sandpiper, on the other hand, midway in size between a Dunlin and a Reeve, has crossed the Atlantic more frequently, and, as over seventy records exist, there is just the possibility that one day we might get the surprise of our lives and add another record to a growing list. It is well to make a note of this, and to remember, if we can, that the markings on its plumage lend to it a characteristic striped effect, and that these markings, ending abruptly halfway down its breast, give the impression of a dusky gorget. Moreover, it has yellowish legs. A near relative, the Siberian Pectoral Sandpiper, has occurred only four times. It is similar to the previous species but lacks the gorget. Its interest to the ornithologist lies in the fact that it is one of the two British waders whose nest and eggs are still unknown. Baird's Sandpiper and Bonaparte's Sandpiper are two more Dunlin-sized American vagrants that have strayed a very few times over to this country. About twenty records exist of the Buff-Breasted Sandpiper, which belongs to a family that is distinguished by having small black spots on the inner sides of its primary feathers. It is a strikingly handsome little bird. As its name implies, its breast and underparts are a warm buff colour, and its legs are orange. It spends the winter in the Argentine, where it gave much pleasure to W. H. Hudson in his early youth. The Broad-Billed Sandpiper is a European species that nests in Norway and Sweden, and it is strange that only a score of records exist for this country. Resembling a small Dunlin with shorter legs and a broader bill, it could be very easily overlooked. In the summer the pattern on its back is unlike that of any other Sandpiper, for it has very dark, Snipe-like pencilled shadings on its plumage. In the winter it is said to be possible to identify it by its white throat and eye-stripe. At least there could be no mistaking the Terek Sandpiper, another north European and Asiatic species. It is extremely improbable that one will come our way, as only seven records exist, but it would be a red-letter day if we should have a view of this miniature Redshank with a bill upcurved like an Avocet, for that is the best description of him that I can think of for impressing his individuality on the mind. Closely related to our Common Sandpiper is the Spotted Sandpiper, a very rare wanderer from America whose occurrence here has been admitted a dozen or more times. It is like the Common Sandpiper, but has round black spots on its underparts. The Solitary Sandpiper, another North American species, is like a smaller edition of our Green Sandpiper without its white rump. Three other rarities remain to be considered, and two of them are more like Redshanks than Sandpipers. The Marsh-Sandpiper, with its slender legs and bill, is like a smaller edition of the Greenshank in winter plumage with all its features almost etherialised by slenderness. It is an east European species which has strayed to Britain to receive a charge of shot some half-dozen times. The Grey-Rumped Sandpiper, similar in size to a Redshank but shorter in the leg, is distinguished by uniformly grey upper parts and dull yellow legs. Its American counterpart is called the Wandering Tattler, and its eggs, for long undiscovered, have now been found on shingle-beds or gravel-bars in dried-up river beds above the timber line. No doubt the Grey-Rumped Sandpiper nests in similar localities in the Alpine zone north of Lake Baikal, but as yet it has eluded the searchers. Two birds of this species have been recorded in Britain, and that is the measure of its rarity as a British species.

Bartram's Sandpiper is the last of the extreme rarities to be noted. Some

Purple Sandpiper dozing on a breakwater at high-tide

thirteen of these have strayed from the American continent and found their way into our records. It is a solitary bird of the open pampas, and it belies its appearance as a Sandpiper by behaving like a Plover. It has the general colouration and size of a Reeve, but its bill and legs are rather shorter. Its neck is slender and its tail noticeably long, and the undersides of its wings are strongly barred.

And so we come to the five Sandpipers that are left, the five that we stand a reasonable chance of seeing in their appropriate seasons every year in this country.

The Purple Sandpiper (which is really of the Dunlin-Stint family) is elusive on the south coast, but readily encountered on both east and west coasts, especially further north. It is typically a bird of the inter-tidal zone on rocky shores, and loves to haunt the barnacle-covered rocks at the edge of the tide, where it keeps company with Turnstones and is not slow to profit from their industry. Its portly little form is readily recognised, and, as it rarely forsakes its beloved rocks and no other waders except Turnstones habitually frequent such places, identification is not very difficult. Its plumage is sombre, but in the right light a purplish gloss can be detected, and hence its name. The darkness of its plumage is relieved by a pair of bright

Common Sandpiper about to brood

Stanton Whitaker

yellow legs. It is the ambition of ornithologists to find its nest in this country, but though occasional birds pass the summer on the northern coastline, it has not yet been proved to breed there. Its breeding-range is very nearly circum-polar, extending from arctic Canada through Greenland, Iceland, Spitzbergen to the Taimyr Peninsula. Its most southerly breeding-haunt is the Faeroes. It nests on the tundra, or further north, amongst mosses near the shore, and when disturbed it slips from its nest and slithers through the undergrowth like a rat.

The Curlew-Sandpiper has already been described with the Dunlin in the section devoted to these two species, and further comment is not necessary here, beyond a caveat to the watcher in the estuary not to assume that all the small, scurrying waders on the mud flats in early autumn are inevitably Dunlins and Sanderlings. The Curlew-Sandpiper may be in their midst and can so easily be overlooked. It is well to remember that its decurved bill and its legs are a little longer than the Dunlin's; its form is more slender and its carriage more upright. Above all remember to look for the white rump as it speeds away.

The Common Sandpiper should be familiar to all, for it lives up to its name, and, except in the south-east of England, it breeds almost everywhere in suitable localities in the British Isles. With the Grey Wagtail and the Dipper, it loves fast-flowing rivers and streams, though it is not confined to such haunts. The Summer Snipe, as it is often called, arrives in April and stays until October, though most birds have departed by the middle of

J. E. Sluiters

Wood-Sandpiper standing in shallow water

September. With brownish-grey upper parts and greyish-white belly, it bobs along by the water's edge, and, if disturbed, it flies off low over the water with a shrill ' twee-wee-wee ' and a very typical jerky wing-action. In late July and August the coastal marshes awaken to life with the shrill, incessant twittering of Sandpipers on the first stage of a southward journey that may take them past the Cape to the East Indies and even Australasia.

If at that time of the year you are exploring the muddy fringes of a lagoon or a marsh fairly near the coast, and a rather larger, longer-legged Sandpiper takes to the air with an excited 'chiff-chiff-chiff' cry, you may be watching, possibly for the first time, a Wood-Sandpiper. It is a bird well worth seeing. To distinguish this species from the Common and Green Sandpipers it is worth noting that in flight the undersides of its wings are greyish, not blackish, and its whitish rump is conspicuous but not startlingly so. In the north European forest belt this is the commonest of the Sandpipers. It usually nests on the ground, but when the forest land is flooded it shows considerable resource in depositing its eggs in the old nests of Fieldfares and other birds, a practice habitually adopted by the Green Sandpiper. I like Miss M. D. Haviland's

J. V. Vijverberg

Green Sandpiper

account of her encounter with a Wood-Sandpiper on its nest. "I was climbing up to what appeared to be a Fieldfare's nest, when, unexpectedly, a long beak like a bee's sting darted over the brim, and instead of the original architect, the grey poll of a Wood-Sandpiper popped up." One would give a lot for an experience of that kind, especially if a camera was at hand.

The Green Sandpiper is of more frequent occurrence than the previous species. It is more an inland bird, and this fact alone is a pointer to its identity, for apart from the Common Sandpiper small waders are not generally found by the edges of inland streams. It is larger, stouter and considerably darker than the Common Sandpiper, and when it is flushed its general appearance is conspicuously black and white. It is almost as if a limicoline House Martin had taken to the air. This impression is conveyed by a pure white rump, tail and belly which contrast strongly with the bird's dark upper parts and the blackish undersides of its wings. It rises high in the air with a 'tweet-weet-weet' cry that is less piercing in tone than the Wood-Sandpiper's excited 'chiff-chiff-chiff.' It is quite extraordinarily faithful to its chosen ditches or streams. Day after day one can go to the same spot and flush what is presumably the same bird. It is a very frequent visitor to sewage farms, and its name looms large in their records. It has bred once for certain in this country—in the Lake District in 1917—and there are many more suspected instances of breeding. With unconquerable optimism I look forward to the day when I might conceivably find its nest. I see myself squelching through an alder thicket and coming across a Thrush's nest in the fork of a lichen-covered tree, and there, peering over the brim of the nest, is a bright-eyed Sandpiper.

In the meantime, it is infinitely more practicable to attempt to secure its portrait by the edge of one of its favourite dikes, which I fully intend to do when next the opportunity presents itself.

19

Redshank, Spotted Redshank and Greenshank

THE Redshank carries a heavier burden of curses on his dappled grey back than any other bird in the estuary. Sooner or later every wildfowler experiences the bitter disappointment of seeing his carefully stalked quarry stampede into flight when a 'shanker' springs up from a hidden creek and retreats yelping over the mud-flats. As watchdog of the estuary he has no equal. Well has he earned the title of 'Warden of the Marshes.' But there is an hour when the Warden may be found off-duty; when for a brief period he can relax his vigilance. At high-tide, if he does not slip off inland to some secluded meadow, he will seek the refuge of a sand-bar or reef of rocks that alone will not be covered by the rising flood. It is then that he can stand at ease, and there, if due precautions are taken and the conditions of tide and weather are favourable, the estuary photographer may interview him, and I know of no experience which can give more satisfaction than to have a throng of these excitable waders moving steadily nearer to the hide, their prancing red legs gleaming in the sunshine, and their yodellings and pipings filling the air with riotous sound. When the water gets too deep for them they will not hesitate to swim fifty yards or more to another reef of rocks, but mostly they like to stand in the shallows with the water washing around their feet. And if, when the high-tide hour is past, they squat on the warm rocks or balance on one leg in sleepy repose, there is a good deal of sly satisfaction in photographing them caught thus, surprisingly, off their guard.

In the last few years there has been a most gratifying increase in the number of Redshanks that frequent the estuaries with which I am familiar. An enquiry into the status of the Redshank conducted by the British Trust for Ornithology has shown that it has been steadily increasing its range during the present century all over Britain. This increase dates from about 1865, and today it has successfully colonised every county, Cornwall and Pembroke excepted, and it bids fair to rank as Britain's most prosperous wader.

The ceremonies that attend the Redshank's courtship are of such surpassing beauty as to demand the pen of an artist to describe them, and the insight of a trained scientist to elicit their interpretation. J. S. Huxley has performed

Eight Redshanks and a lone Dunlin on a sea-washed reef

the latter service, and his observations and deductions may be read in *A First Account of the Courtship of the Redshank* (*Proc. Zool. Soc.*, 1912, pp. 647-55). Of the many artistic accounts of the ceremonies that exist I like none better than H. J. Massingham's, for it seems to me exactly to convey the enchantment of a scene that anyone may be privileged to witness one spring morning in the water meadows where the Redshanks nest. " Some thirty or forty birds will rise into the air, and oblivious to all dangers and disharmonies, sway into their nuptial songs and dances. One by one they stop dead in the air, with wings depressed, partridge-fashion, when they sheer the top of the hedge into the pasture beyond. Holding their bodies rigid and sustained, they fall into a kind of plainsong with regular beats. For a time they hang suspended thus, with drooping and vibrating wings, and then, either plumb or diagonally, begin to sink. Some fall but a few feet, others nearly reach the ground. Suddenly the wings are shivered and pulsated with such insect-like rapidity that the body is forced upwards without the wings being raised above

Spotted Red-
shanks forag-
ing—winter
dress

F. P. J. Kooymans

its level, and once more they top the brow of the air slope and in stooping duck-poise hang there. When the dips are short, the bird travels in waves; when near the ground, in broad curves. Rarely do they come to earth while the ritual lasts, but when they do, the continuity of the love-dance is maintained by the lover mincing over to his mate with wings lifted, arched and quivering to display their silvery white and melt her to their beauty."

When the eggs are laid and the sitting bird has twined the grass-stems into

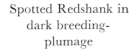

Spotted Redshank in
dark breeding-
plumage

J. V. Vijverberg

108

a green bower over her head, much of the excitement dies down, though out-
breaks may occur from time to time. Brooding Redshanks show remarkably
different temperaments in the face of a hide and a photographer. I have
known birds so wild that it would have been disastrous to attempt to accustom
them to a camera. Others are so possessed with maternity that they will

F. P. J. Kooymans

Greenshank—a photograph that does full justice
to the bird's winter plumage

allow themselves to be lifted off the eggs by hand. The Redshank is the only
wader that I have had to remove gently but forcibly from her eggs in order to
photograph her in a more attractive position.

Occasionally in spring, but more regularly in autumn, the watcher on the
marshes may see a small party of birds that are obviously of the 'shanker'
type, but with certain strongly marked characteristics of their own. He should

note well the features of these transitory visitors, for it may be a long time before he will chance to see them again, for the Spotted or Dusky Redshank is a bird of infrequent occurrence. In the spring there can be no mistaking him, for no other wader of his size has that cloak of sooty black relieved by small white flecks. The legs are a very deep orange-red, so dark in the spring as almost to appear black, and the bill, too, is darkly hued.

In the autumn the Spotted Redshank has an ashy-grey appearance, but its larger size, relatively longer bill and the absence of white secondaries should help to distinguish it from the Redshank. The barring on its scapulars and the generally white-spotted appearance of its upper parts should serve to separate it from the Greenshank. Its flight-note, a disyllabic ' tchuet,' is quite unlike that of the other two species, and once heard is never forgotten. A bird of the northern forest belt, its nest was first discovered by John Wolley in Finland in 1853. He found it in clearings that had been brought about by forest fires. Amongst the charred logs in this sombre setting the bird's dusky plumage found a most appropriate background. It does not always resort to such sites, and subsequent nests have been found in green marshes and cloud-berry bogs. I am indebted to F. P. J. Kooymans and to J. V. Vijverberg for the accompanying photographs which show the Spotted Redshank in both summer and winter plumage. They were taken in Holland, where the bird turns up on migration with rather more frequency than is the case in this country. I believe it has yet to be photographed for the first time in England.

The Greenshank is a taller, larger and greyer bird than the Redshank, with relatively longer legs of a pale olive-green, and its bill has a slight but decided upward tilt to it. It has no white on the wing either when standing or in flight, in marked contrast with the Redshank, whose most characteristic feature in flight is the broad white crescent on the hind border of its wing. The Greenshank makes up for absence of white on the wing by showing a very conspicuous white rump and pale tail in flight. Its call-note, a loud, clear ' tew, tew, tew,' is lower in pitch and less musical than the Redshank's. As a breeding species the Greenshank is just holding its own, though confined to the northern parts of Scotland and some of the outer islands, but it is a comparative rarity and deserving of rigorous protection. Our best chances of seeing Greenshanks is when they make their leisurely progress southwards at the end of the summer, for they follow inland routes and are frequent visitors to reservoirs and sewage farms or the banks of quiet rivers.

The Greenshank is reserved and rather sedate, or perhaps appears so because we compare him with his exceedingly volatile cousin. But he is not given to the agitated ducking action so typical of the Redshank, and he appears to go quietly about his business without concerning himself with his neighbours' affairs. He is not 'Jealous in honour, sudden and quick in quarrel.' He has slipped quietly from the Fourth into the Fifth Age, where formality takes the place of impetuosity. 'And so he plays his part'— and a very welcome part too, for the Greenshanks that I have seen have always matched their surroundings with great dignity and grace. They confirm one's belief that waders have a perfection of form which is not granted in such generous measure to other birds. One feels that a Greenshank, wherever he found himself, would never look undignified or out of place.

T. M. Fowler

Greenshank brooding

20

Ringed Plover, Kentish Plover and Little Ringed Plover

A FEW acres of fairly unfrequented beach anywhere along the coastline of Great Britain, and that is all a pair of Ringed Plovers ask for themselves; and there they will rear their family and risk the week-end trippers and the early morning bathers who crunch their way over the shingles totally oblivious of the four eggs that lie amongst the pebbles, open to the sky above but concealed by a miracle of protective colouration so effective that even if you know the whereabouts of a nest, you may stand within a few paces of it and search your hardest and still it eludes your questing eyes. Long and lonely dune-fringed shores are the Ringed Plover's favourite haunts, but I know a stretch of shingle near a busy harbour mouth, where smoke and acrid fumes from factories near-by make foul the air; where men and ships come and go all day long, and there a pair of Ringed Plovers lay their eggs, and as often as not, rear their family with success. And I call to mind a little sandy bay hollowed in the Pembrokeshire cliffs by centuries of Atlantic gales, and there, cut off from contact with their nearest kindred by mile upon mile of sheer cliff, were two Ringed Plovers—and they had a nest with eggs on the shell-strewn margin of the beach. In some localities the Ringed Plover will penetrate far inland, and on the Breckland in Norfolk I have seen it in Stone Curlew country quite as much at home as if it were on the fore-shore fifty miles away.

There are always a few Ringed Plovers that assemble with other waders at a high-tide roost, but they do not display the same clannishness as other waders, and their restlessness compels them to wander about hither and thither amongst the other birds. They always seem to sense when the camera is turned in their direction, for suspicion is writ large in their eyes, and they bob about and make little stooping runs, and, in fact, are very trying subjects indeed.

There is no difficulty in recognising the Ringed Plover at once from the other small waders whose company it shares. He is like a dumpy little gentleman who has strayed out of a Victorian novel, complete with sandy-brown jacket, white forehead and temples, and an even whiter collar and shirt front

Arnold H. Smith

Ringed Plover brooding on the open beach

which make a fine contrast with his black cravat. When feeding on the flats he toddles along, halts, changes direction, toddles on again, halts—and so it goes on with endless variations. In flight the wings are pointed, and a narrow white bar shows clearly, and when a Ringed Plover alights he does so with wings uplifted and little feet twinkling along beneath him. Juvenile birds in the early autumn have a duller appearance than their parents, and the dark cravat of maturity is not fully formed, so that an inexperienced watcher may think he has in view the far rarer Kentish Plover. Inspection of the legs will quickly settle any doubts. The young Ringed Plover has yellowish legs, not, it is true, as startlingly yellow as its parents', but yellow for all that. The Kentish Plover's legs are black in every stage of growth, and that one single difference will always settle any doubts.

The Kentish Plover is a rare bird, some would say an exceedingly rare bird, in this country, though common enough when you cross the Channel. The isolated colony in Kent is on the verge of extinction. If two or three pairs of birds successfully rear their young in a season it is surprising, and quite possibly by now the bird has ceased to exist as a resident species. Out of the nesting-season it is a rare migrant on the spring and autumn passage. The chances of encountering it at high tide in the estuary are so remote that I had never given the bird more than a passing thought until, one day in late April, when I was feverishly focusing on two Grey Plovers that had arrived and were standing in shallow water fifteen yards from the hide, I saw a

Female Kentish Plover at nest

J. E. Sluiters

Kentish Plover's unmistakable image appear lower down on the focusing screen. I was so surprised that I let fly the shutter without altering the band of focus, and before I had time to wind on the film and collect my wits all the birds in the group—two Grey Plovers, a Kentish Plover, a Ringed Plover and two Dunlins—had departed. A fortnight later, when the next suitable tide occurred, I went to the island again, and to my delight the Kentish Plover again arrived, and, though he insisted on sheltering behind a party of somnolent Dunlins, I was able to record his image in a way that leaves no doubt about his identity. I wonder how many years will pass before I see my next Kentish Plover? Smaller, paler, slighter and more sandy-brown than the Ringed Plover, its distinguishing features are the dark patches on either side of its breast instead of the continuous black band of the Ringed Plover. In the female these dark patches are often so slight as to be hardly discernible. The white patch on the bird's forehead continues over the eye, giving the impression that the narrow dark band below it runs continuously 'through' the eye. The male has a dark mark above the white forehead, but this is lacking in the female. As previously mentioned, black legs distinguish the Kentish Plover at all seasons.

Considerable interest was aroused in ornithological circles in this country, when a pair of Little Ringed Plovers were found to have nested by a Hertford-

Male Kentish Plover resting with Dunlins during the high-tide

shire reservoir in 1938. A new breeding species was added to the British list, though whether this was a purely freak occurrence was not known at the time. Records showed an increase of this bird on the Continent which seemed to indicate a westward colonising trend. Other pairs of Little Ringed Plovers have appeared in subsequent years in other suitable localities in the home counties and further afield, so that it now seems that we have acquired in the present decade a new breeding species that intends to return here year by year. The Little Ringed Plover is more a fresh-water than a coastal species. It is usually found inland, and has a marked preference for gravel pits and the shingly edges of reservoirs, though it may decide to conduct its domestic affairs on any stretch of waste ground, even in the vicinity of a rubbish-dump. In appearance it is much like the Ringed Plover, but it has a slighter build. In flight it lacks the Ringed Plover's white wing bar, and when on the ground there are two things that distinguish it. Round the eye it has a very bright yellow orbital ring, and on its head, above the black forehead band which the Ringed Plover and the male Kentish Plover both possess, it has a narrow white streak. Its note, too, is distinctive—a thin, higher-pitched note than the Ringed Plover's—a musical ' tee-ū.'

A solitary example of a North American species—the Semi-Palmated

J. E. Sluiters

A new-comer to this country—the Little Ringed Plover at nest

Ringed Plover—found its way into our records in 1916. Very similar in plumage to our native Ringed Plover, it must be an uncommonly difficult bird to separate in the field, but the suggestion of webbing between its toes, from which it derives its name, is diagnostic at all stages of growth.

A smaller, darker form of the Ringed Plover, the Arctic Ringed Plover, appears in Britain as a winter visitor and passage-migrant, but he is a very confident ornithologist who will swear to its identity in the field, for our own Ringed Plovers show variations of size and plumage which can be misleading, and it is safer to give them the benefit of the doubt.

21

Grey and Golden Plover

A wader quiz—six different species in as many square yards. Against a background of Oyster-Catchers are four Grey Plovers, four Bar-Tailed Godwits, three Knots, a Dunlin and a Turnstone

IN the hierarchy of waders both Grey and Golden Plovers belong to the category of 'medium-sized.' Not quite as large as the Godwits, though appreciably bigger than Knots, they are never in danger of being over-looked in the estuary. Turnstones and Dunlins are dwarfed by their presence, but they in their turn look comparatively small—though never insignificant—beside Oyster-Catchers and other larger wading birds.

It is a rare coincidence of time and place, of tide and weather, which will enable one to see, let alone photograph, these differences of size in a single grouping of birds, and I look back with singular satisfaction to that blustery March day when, in the space of a few square yards, I had Grey Plovers standing shoulder to shoulder with five other wader species, and all of them visible on my focusing screen at the same time.

In winter dress Grey and Golden Plovers are not easily separable from one another. Both display the same subtle harmony of grey and white, and though the Golden Plover is less robust than the Grey, this difference in size is not an easy guide to recognition when you are looking at birds through glasses at a range of a hundred yards or more. Grey Plovers usually feed in

Northern Golden Plover at nest. In 1948 a pair was found nesting on St. Kilda in company with birds of the southern form, and a new breeding-bird was thus added to the British List

small parties or as isolated individuals, and they appear almost to avoid the near proximity of their neighbours on the flats. Golden Plovers are far more sociably inclined, and when they feed on tidal mud they seem to regard the occasion as one for displaying their noticeably more gregarious tendencies. But they are not confined, as are Grey Plovers, to mud flats and saltings. They are almost more at home on inland fallows and grassland, where they share the company of Lapwings and Skylarks, and indulge in occasional bursts of aerial display which have a singular charm and beauty. When they alight again each bird will reveal for a moment after alighting the light undersides of its wings, as if to say: " Mark well my silvery arm-pits lest you confuse me with my cousin on the flats." For, hidden under their wings, both Grey and Golden Plovers carry the secrets of their identity. When the Grey Plover lifts its wings you see at once its black axillaries, and, in flight, these dusky patches wink darkly at you as the birds fly past. The call-notes of the two species are also distinctive. The Golden Plover whistles a melodious ' tlui '; the Grey Plovers a trisyllabic ' tlee-oo-ee,' higher in pitch and wilder in tone.

F. P. J. Kooymans

Grey Plover in full breeding-plumage

In nuptial dress there can be no confusion between the two species. The Golden Plover richly earns its name, for its back is a glory of barred and spangled golden-yellow, and the white fringe to its black waistcoat gives it a great air of distinction. Birds of the northern race of Golden Plover which are noted here on passage in late spring have all these markings far more strongly emphasized.

But the Grey Plover in summer dress—what a miracle of transformation is effected here! Words cannot adequately convey the glory of his chequered silver back, the startling whiteness of his brow and shoulders, and the sheer blackness of his frontal facings—'a deep but dazzling darkness' which extends right under his belly until it ends with a shimmer of white at his rump. I shall never rest content until I have photographed him in the wild in the full splendour of his nuptial attire. I have had a bird almost in range one May day in the estuary. The rising tide edged him nearer and nearer, but the wildness of the north was in his veins, and when he was still fifty yards away he suddenly took his departure with that wild and plaintive whistle which is one of the most endearing of all sounds to those who know the saltings and love the feathered folk that sojourn there.

On the tundras of the high north Grey Plovers make their nests, and Little Stints are there to keep them company. Golden Plovers are not so elusive, for they may be found nesting on high moorlands in this country, and there Dunlins play page to them in their nesting-haunts.

119   I

Golden Plover in its moorland breeding-haunt

Seebohm and Harvie-Brown first discovered the Grey Plover's breeding-grounds in Siberian Europe in 1875. Suffering the tortures of the damned by reason of the mosquitoes that swarm to an appalling degree in those regions, they lay out on the tundra for hours at a stretch before their patience was rewarded. At least we need not undergo this degree of hardship if we wish to view Grey Plovers in this country, for they are not excessively wild, and will admit a reasonably near approach; but I suspect that many hours of watching and discomfort lie ahead for me before I secure my coveted portrait of this superlative bird in its breeding-plumage. They will not be wasted hours, nor will my waiting be in vain. Changeless but ever-changing in the variety of its wader visitants, the estuary will always breathe its spell, for ' Age cannot wither her, nor custom stale her infinite variety.'

22

The Dotterel

TO call the Dotterel an anachronism is hardly complimentary, but that is what it really is—a courageous survivor of the fauna that repopulated this land when it was recovering from the effects of the last of the Ice Ages. The very few pairs of Dotterels that still nest in Britain are confined to the inhospitable tops of the Cairngorms, Grampians and other isolated ranges

G. K. Yeates

Dotterel brooding

of the central highlands, and, in England, very sparingly to the high fells of the Lake District. Botanists are familiar with the restriction of plant forms to particular zones where temperature and climatic conditions impose their limitations. The Dotterel is a bird with similar restrictions, and just as Alpine plants descend from their cloudy heights the further north we go, so with the Dotterel. In the far north, in Finland, Sweden and Norway, the Dotterel comes down to earth, and though it favours a plateau with a certain elevation, it will quite happily nest near sea-level.

But here, if we wish to interview this bird, we must climb above the three-thousand-foot contour in the central highlands before we reach its haunts, and there in the wind-swept uplands, amongst the lichen-covered granites, we may find its nest, and, if we are fortunate, we may even stroke the bird as she sits there, for the Dotterel is absurdly confiding, a trait which has all too often been the cause of its undoing.

On migration, and more especially in late April and May, small 'trips' of Dotterel work overland along ancestral routes through Britain, but their numbers are small and their arrival of doubtful occurrence. They favour moors and hill-pastures as stopping-places, but are sometimes seen on coastal marshes and inland meadows. They look like smaller editions of the Golden Plover when seen at a distance. But as they are conspicuously tame it should be possible to approach them nearly, when the broad white eye-stripes meeting in the nape, and the peculiar pattern on the breast—chestnut under-parts separated by a white band from the grey-brown throat and chest—should cause no trouble in settling their identity.

'Foolish Dotterel' is the name we have given to this confiding bird, which is really a comment on our own inconsistency, for a trusting disposition in domesticated animals is what we most admire, but the same traits in a bird are regarded as evidence of stupidity. A more enlightened generation may arise who can enjoy watching a confiding bird without wishing to slay it. I am afraid that in the Dotterel's case they may arrive too late.

23

Black-Winged Stilt and Avocet

G. K. Yeates

Black-Winged Stilts. The female is about to relieve the male

THE inclusion of these two birds, which might well have strayed into the pages of a British bird book from out of some old Chinese tapestry, would be necessary if only to follow the time-honoured tradition of praising those birds that we have tried our hardest, by the medium of the gun and the collector's cabinet, to banish from our shores. But in the last five years each of these remarkable birds has repaid the ingratitude of centuries by nesting again in these islands, and it is a tribute to the latter-day enlightenment of our people that they have done so successfully in spite of the hosts of Midian that prowled and prowled around.

The Black-Winged Stilt, a cosmopolitan species which ranges the world from southern Europe to Asia, from Africa to Ceylon, has been aptly described as a kind of aerial spider-bird. It has enormously long, thin pink legs which trail far behind it in flight, and its bill is a long, thin needle. Its plumage is just sheer black and white, by which I mean that whereas most black-and-white birds have tricksy bits of shading here and there, the adult Stilt is either one thing or the other. No other wader has such bold, decisive contrast.

It may not seem altogether fitting to associate this etherial creature with a sewage farm, for a sewage farm is not a place with a great æsthetic appeal; but it is food and quietude and not æsthetic surroundings that appeal to birds, and from their point of view the deposition of sludge into settling tanks which are taken in rotation has great advantages. The larvæ of small flies in their millions inhabit the tanks and filter-beds, and these tiny scavengers perform a useful service in devouring organic matter and in cleaning the clinkers. They also provide an easy food supply for any waders that are passing that way, or who may care to take up their quarters there for a time.

It was a Nottingham sewage farm that received a party of Black-Winged Stilts in the spring of 1945, a year that saw a remarkable invasion of our country by these birds—an invasion probably not unconnected with events on the Continent during those historic days. Five other counties, widely separated, reported odd birds that year, and in Devon no less than ten Stilts were seen. But it was Nottingham that made history, for three pairs of birds made nests in the precincts of the sewage farm, and though one clutch of eggs was taken in ignorance by a local boy and all did not go well with another nest, four eggs were hatched and three young Stilts were successfully reared for the first time in the annals of British ornithology.

A similar story can be told of the Avocet, though here we have a bird which bred in former days in large colonies in most east and south-eastern counties. The taking of its eggs for food and the drainage of the fens eventually led to its extermination as a breeding-species just over a century ago, but it still visits us as a migrant and is of sparse though fairly regular occurrence. Its long upcurved bill, in shape like a saddler's awl, and the striking pattern of black barrings on snow-white plumage, make the bird unmistakable, though at a distance, in company with Black-Headed Gulls, it could be overlooked.

After the lapse of a century, in 1938, two pairs nested in Ireland, a remarkable occurrence when it is considered that the Avocet has only been recorded about twenty times from that country. But better things were in store, for in the summer of 1947, in two adjacent localities in East Anglia, small colonies of Avocets established themselves, and nine pairs of adult birds were present during the breeding-season, of which at least seven pairs nested. Altogether sixteen young birds were known to have reached the free-flying state. The site is one which presents reasonable opportunities for preservation, and with

G. des Forges

Avocet

the co-operation of the landowners concerned and under the ægis of the Royal Society for the Protection of Birds there seems a very good chance that the Avocet will once again take its rightful place as a British breeding species. Rumours of other Avocets seen prospecting for nesting territories suggest that the species is seeking to extend its range. The colonies in Holland, where an enlightened people afford the bird full protection, may be sending their surplus over to our shores. Whether we deserve this bounty will be seen by the effective measures we take to see that these honoured visitors—these would-be residents—are, as far as possible, afforded security from their natural enemies, and full protection from those miserable kleptomaniacs the egg-collectors, and from the irresponsible man with a gun who will shoot any bird that he sees because it happens to be beautiful and rare.

24

The Lapwing

THERE must be very many bird lovers who, because they live far inland and never get a chance to visit wader haunts along the coastline, are wistfully ignorant of the species that are of everyday occurrence there; for whom Knot, Godwit and Turnstone are legendary figures glimpsed only in the coloured plates of a bird book. But he is an unfortunate person indeed who has not, within fairly easy reach of his home, a meadow or a stretch of ploughland over which an April Lapwing cries and tumbles through the air in the sheer exuberance of spring, for of all our resident waders the Lapwing is still, though now in sadly diminished numbers, the commonest species. And there are few sights that for sheer loveliness can compare with the display flight of a Lapwing on an April day, when cloud shadows race across the meadows and sudden tempestuous showers alternate with bursts of brilliant sunshine, and all the world is young. See him rise from the ground with slow measured beats of his great rounded wings; watch him quicken the pace, rise abruptly in an almost vertical climb, and as suddenly plunge down, twisting and turning as though out of control, and then, a few inches from the ground—so near that his sitting mate will flinch—he sweeps off with a side-to-side tilting flight, and the rasp of his wing-beats comes loud and clear; and over all the countryside resounds his glad spring cry: 'Peer...wit-wit... peer-wit.'

In the distance a Lapwing is a black-and-white bird with an elevated crest. At closer quarters one can see that he is not black at all, but has upper parts of a rare metallic green shot with purple. True, his crest is black and so is his bib which stands out in strong contrast with his white facial patches and underparts. A splash of chestnut under his tail is a colourful afterthought.

The Lapwing's year, like the schoolboy's, is divided into three terms of roughly similar duration. The first and slightly the longest lasts from February until mid-June. It is then that the chosen acre exerts its homing influence upon the birds, and, often in close proximity with other pairs of Lapwings and sometimes within a few yards of Redshanks, they lay their eggs, and trust that they will escape the attentions of their many enemies, from chain harrows to Carrion Crows; from egg collectors to browsing cattle.

Lapwing approaching nest

The second phase begins in June and overlaps to some extent with the first. A gradual assembly of birds takes place, often at no great distance from their breeding-grounds, and flocks of from fifty to two hundred and fifty birds, old and young, feed together in the fields, shift about a certain amount, but show a considerable degree of stability. In the early autumn this phase gives way to a third in which sudden nomadic movements over large areas are frequent, and often involve flocks of several hundreds or even thousands of Lapwings. Sometimes these movements are in the form of a definite overseas migration; sometimes they are just weather movements; sometimes less explicable wanderings are undertaken because there is a spirit of restlessness abroad. The ringing of British-born Lapwings shows that with our birds migration is largely individual. Some Lapwings are sedentary, others disperse locally, and the recovery of ringed birds abroad seems to point to about three-fifths of our birds migrating to France, Spain, Portugal and occasionally further south and east. Continental Lapwings that winter here arrive in mid-autumn mostly from countries round the Baltic. In 1927 a party of Lapwings migrating from England to Ireland failed to strike their objective and were carried by an easterly gale across the Atlantic, eventually making a land-fall in Newfoundland and on the coast of Labrador, where, mindful of the country of their origin and its reputation for Empire-building, they proceeded to settle down and found a new colony. By a happy chance—and one which alone would justify the years of endeavour behind the British Birds Ringing Scheme—one of these birds bore a ring on its leg which showed that it had been hatched out in Cumberland.

The Lapwing is essentially a bird of the soil, and almost alone amongst birds, it has been acknowledged as wholly beneficial to agriculture at every season of the year. The farmer who finds a Lapwing's nest and refrains from taking the eggs, delicacy though they be, does so today, not only out of respect for an Act of Parliament, but because he realises that in the Lapwing he has an ally who will account for innumerable wireworms and leather-jackets as long as it is welcomed as a guest.

It is generally considered that the bird has made a recovery in numbers since the passing of the Lapwing Act in 1926, but my observations of breeding birds in Sussex do not bear out this opinion. Every year there are fewer birds, and places on the Downs and in the water meadows which are still known locally as ' Plover Grounds ' now hardly boast more than an isolated pair of birds. Where the country people used to go with baskets to collect their eggs the Lapwings are now no more, and the countryside is infinitely the poorer for their departure. A water-meadow in April without Lapwings tumbling in the air has lost more than half its sparkle and charm.

25

The Oyster-Catcher

THE estuary photographer has good reason to be grateful to the Oyster-Catcher, for not only is it a dependable bird that always turns up in good time at a high-tide roost, but it acts as a splendid decoy to other more wary waders who would not pay their fleeting visits at all were it not for the confidence inspired in them by the presence of this garrulous creature who has a breezy, self-reliant manner which is calculated to put courage into the most faint-hearted. The Oyster-Catcher's pied livery and orange-red bill are always worth photographing for their own sake, even though its pink legs are submerged in water as they so often are, for the Oyster-Catcher loves nothing more than to stand in the shallows and provide a suitable background for the smaller waders grouped on the shingles in front of him. I must possess hundreds of negatives which include Oyster-Catchers somewhere in the background, but there are occasions when odd groups of birds stray near the hide or pose on deeply shadowed rocks by the water's edge, and the temptation to photograph them is always irresistible. I have also wasted a lot of film trying to record the dazzling beauty of their flight, and many a time—but only once successfully—have I tried to photograph them swimming, for Oyster-Catchers, like most waders, are not averse to taking to the water when the occasion demands it.

But what I most enjoy is to lie concealed on an island in a western estuary when the winter assemblage of these birds is complete; to be surrounded, not by scores or even hundreds, but by thousands of Oyster-Catchers, all crowding in on the hide, piping and kleeping at the tops of their voices, jostling one another for positions of advantage, and finally settling down to slumber, orange bills tucked away deeply into scapulars, and hardly a sound coming from the assembled host. An account of this experience has already been given and it calls for no further comment here beyond saying again that for one who has been starved of winged company there can be no more satisfying experience.

When the New Year is not very far advanced the Oyster-Catcher flocks begin to disintegrate, and small parties find their way to breeding-

Oyster-Catchers in silhouette

haunts all round the coast of Britain, and, particularly in the north, far inland up river valleys.

Pairs go off to their breeding-sites long before nesting begins, and they spend a portion of the day there before returning to the flocks at other times. It is then that the Oyster-Catcher's ceremonial 'piping performance' can be observed. It is a ritual that is undertaken by two or more birds—often in parties of up to a dozen—and is continued long after the breeding season. With necks thrust forward, shoulders elevated, and bills down-pointing, they run around in curves or not infrequently spin round on the same spot, frantically piping the while. The significance of this display has been interpreted by T. S. Huxley and F. A. Montague in an interesting paper contributed to the *Ibis* (1925, Series 12, vol. 1, p. 868). More recently, experimental work with a stuffed Oyster-Catcher in a breeding territory has resulted in a series of interesting photographs by Stuart Smith and Eric Hosking.

It is amusingly appropriate that this colourful harlequin of a bird should have been misnamed from the start, for it is edible mussels and not oysters that are its principal diet. An analysis of mussel shells successfully attacked and emptied of their contents by Oyster-Catchers was made by J. M. Dewar (*Zoologist*, 1908). He found that 78 per cent of mussels were split open through the dorsal border, 9 per cent through the ventral border, and 13 per cent through the posterior end. Small mussels were swallowed whole.

Oyster-Catchers in August. Two birds are already in winter plumage

This resourceful bird is not solely dependent on the mussel beds for its food supply. Crustaceans, worms and insects are welcome additions to its diet, and there are records of it eating eggs and even young birds. But aberrations of this kind are exceptional and perhaps excusable in so highly individual a bird, for there are hidden depths in that smouldering red eye of his that are still to be explored.

26

The Stone-Curlew

THE Stone-Curlew, which has affinities with the crane group and more particularly with the bustards, is included amongst the British waders with the same sort of mental reservations that we unconsciously adopt with people of other nationalities who become British subjects. But no one who has seen this bullet-headed, plover-like bird skulking over the downland could ever doubt that its form and its whole pattern of behaviour resemble that of many other wader species. The name Curlew is an unfortunate misnomer, for it has few things in common with that bird, except its love of solitary places and a certain haunting wildness in its cry. Norfolk Plover is a more appropriate name, though even this implies a limitation of range which is misleading, for there are probably more people who have seen this bird on the chalky uplands of southern England than on the flinty Breckland of Norfolk. Today its range is severely limited to certain desolate tracts of country in the south and south-east of England. A century ago it was not an uncommon bird on the wolds of Lincolnshire and Yorkshire and even further north, but it will not tolerate the intrusion of man into its haunts. It must have wide horizons, and in Norfolk today the introduction of conifer plantations to its breeding-grounds is likely to have an increasingly unsettling effect on its sensitive disposition. In the south country much of the downland is coming under the plough, and this, too, is likely to affect the local distribution if not the actual status of this fastidious bird.

In Sussex it is in the last week of March that we climb up to the Downs in the hope of seeing our first Stone-Curlews, newly arrived from their African winter quarters. Then, we are fortunate if we glimpse a solitary pair of birds. In September it is not unusual to see a dozen or more of them skulking about together on the fringes of gorse thickets. At this season the Stone-Curlew unexpectedly reveals a gregarious side to its nature.

On its breeding-grounds it is more often heard than seen, and then chiefly towards dusk, for it is a bird of crepuscular habits, and it is when darkness is falling over the bare downland that its weird wailing cries begin to be heard; or on moonlight nights when the birds call like the disembodied spirits of the ancient past, for Stone-Curlews love the flint-strewn country where the hut-

Stone-Curlew—a stealthy approach to the nesting-site

sites and lynchets of early man excite the interest of historians today. It was there, amongst the flints disturbed by an archæologist's spade, that I found my first Stone-Curlew's nest—a setting curiously appropriate to a bird which has set its face against the march of progress and which can only live its solitary life remote and apart.

On those dry and barren uplands, where dew ponds are the only means that man has contrived for conserving a barely adequate supply of water for the sheep that pasture there, the Stone-Curlew finds its sustenance. Snails and slugs are its staple food, though insects are also eaten and an occasional vole or field-mouse does not come amiss. Exceedingly cautious at the nest, like all birds it can be accustomed to a photographer's hide if due precautions are taken, and when the eggs are hatching it becomes positively tame. I found that nothing short of a personal appearance from the hide would make it leave its chicks when they were lying helpless in the nesting-scrape. But this phase quickly passes, for the young are running with their parents a few hours after emerging from the eggs. Then, if they are caught unawares on the open down, they freeze into perfect immobility, and they are uncommonly difficult to detect as they lie with necks outstretched, their grey and sandy astrakhan down matching to perfection the flinty waste-land against which they have flattened themselves. I retain one ineradicable memory of my acquaintance with the Stone-Curlew at the nest—the baleful amber of its staring eyes. No bird of my acquaintance has quite such disconcerting power concentrated in its gaze. It looks at you and through you to limitless horizons beyond, and as an intruder on its privacy in that lonely place it makes you feel—well, just a shade uncomfortable.

British Waders in Flight

K

Three Plates by Basil Laker

Some time ago I had occasion to visit a well-known Bird Museum in Brighton, and I was greatly interested to watch there an artist who was sketching with scrupulous care a stuffed seagull. It seemed a little odd to me that he should be so employed, with living gulls flying in the air or perching on the Pier a mile away. I did not stop to point this out to him as I do not think my observations would have been particularly well received, but I made a mental note that if ever I wanted an artist to illustrate any material of mine he would not be one who drew his inspiration from a museum specimen.

Not long afterwards, on one of my visits to the estuary, I found that a new hide had sprung up, as it were overnight, on the island where I intended to spend the high-tide hours. Its occupant was a young man who was, I suspect, not a little disconcerted to find that he was not alone in his quest for solitude and the companionship of the birds that would shortly throng the island. I imagined that he, too, was preparing for a seven-hour vigil in order to record in photographic form the wader visitors to the island, but, to my surprise, I found that he was equipped with nothing more than a sketch book and a pencil. He allowed me to see some of the drawings that he had made on previous visits to the estuary, and I was so impressed by the spontaneity with which he had recorded, with a few strokes of his pencil, the essential characteristics of waders on the wing, that I asked him if he would do some plates for this book, which was then in its early stages of preparation. He consented to do so, and I can only say that I was delighted with the results. I feel that I can confidently leave others to judge their merit for themselves.

A Purple Sandpiper, B Curlew, C Whimbrel, D Spotted Redshank, E Greenshank, F Redshank, G Avocet, H Black-Winged Stilt, I Reeve, J Oyster-Catcher, K Bar-Tailed Godwit, L Black-Tailed Godwit

A Sanderling (*summer*), B Little Stint, C Temminck's Stint, D Dunlin (*winter*), E Sanderling (*winter*), F Little Ringed Plover, G Dunlin (*summer*), H Curlew-Sandpiper (*summer*), I Curlew-Sandpiper (*winter*), J Knot (*winter*), K Kentish Plover, L Knot (*summer*), M Turnstone, N Golden Plover (*winter*), O Ringed Plover, P Grey Plover (*winter*), Q Grey Plover (*summer*), R Golden Plover (*summer*)

A Great Snipe, B Lapwing, C Dotterel, D Jack Snipe, E Dotterel, F Woodcock, G Snipe, H Green Sandpiper, I Common Sandpiper, J Wood-Sandpiper, K Green Sandpiper, L Stone-Curlew, M Wood-Sandpiper

Supplement

I have attempted to set down here in a concise form the salient features of all the waders that occur with any frequency in Britain. Today, no one would think of attempting such a task without frequent reference to that monumental compendium of observation and knowledge—*The Handbook of British Birds*, by Witherby, Jourdain, Ticehurst and Tucker. I beg to acknowledge my debt to this great work, and to *British Birds*, the monthly magazine which is published under the same auspices and by the same publishing house. The following is the key to the list of abbreviations used:

A Length   B Bill   C Legs
D Plumage and diagnostic
   features
E Call notes
F Display
G Food

H Distribution
J Movements
K Habitat out of nesting season
L Habitat in nesting season
M Nest   N Eggs
O Incubation

BAR-TAILED GODWIT *Limosa lapponica lapponica* (*Linnæus*, 1758)

A   c. 15 ins.   B   Long and straight, slightly upturned at tip. Flesh-coloured. Length variable: 3-4 ins.   C   Greenish-grey.

D   Godwits are the only shore waders with very long, straight bills. Bar-Tailed Godwit's is slightly upcurved at tip. Black-Tailed Godwit's almost completely straight. In summer male Bar-Tailed Godwit has rufous head, neck and underparts. Female generally duller. Juveniles have buff breasts. In winter all birds have streaked grey-brown plumage similar to Curlew's. Can be distinguished from Black-Tailed Godwit by shorter stature, by absence of broad, white wing-bar, and broad black band on otherwise white tail. Barring in tail not conspicuous. In flight feet project only slightly beyond tail.

E   In Britain not particularly vocal. Flight-note a subdued " barking "—" kurrue . . . kurrue." On breeding-grounds very noisy, with great variety of cries.

F   Song flight in breeding-haunts—wings decurved and stiffened, with rapid strokes and glides alternating. Other forms of display not yet sufficiently studied.

G   Essentially insects, small crustacea, mollusca, etc., found on mud flats and in tidal ooze.

H   A N. Palæarctic species, breeding from N. Norway, N.E. Sweden, Finland and Russia to Yenesei and Taimyr. Eastern race breeds in N.E. Siberia to W. Alaska. *British Isles:* Passage-migrant and winter visitor to all coasts, but scarce in extreme north. Seldom found inland. Many non-breeders stay the summer.

J   Typical race migrates from northern breeding-grounds through Europe and W. Asia to Baltic, N. Sea and Atlantic coasts of Europe, Mediterranean, and W. African coast to Senegambia; also east to Black Sea, Arabian and Somali coasts, and shores of Indian Ocean. Eastern race winters Malay, Oceania and Australasia. *British Isles:* N. migration begins March and continues to June (peak period early May); chiefly E. coast. S. migration from mid-July to mid-November; E. and W. coasts.

K   Essentially estuarine. Marked preference for muddy shores and estuaries, though sometimes on sandy shores. Occasional and rare inland.
L   Swampy arctic-tundra beyond or on the edge of tree-limit.
M   Hollow in the ground, lined with lichens, dry leaves, etc., in arctic swamps where occasional ridges afford dry location.   N   Normally 4. Greenish-brown streaked with umber. c. $1\frac{1}{2}$ by $2\frac{1}{10}$ ins.
    O   By both sexes. About 3 weeks, but period not definitely known.

BLACK-TAILED GODWIT *Limosa limosa limosa* (*Linnæus*, 1758)

A   c. 17 ins.   B   Long and straight. Upper part yellowish-pink. Darkens to tip. Very slightly upturned. Length variable. c. $3\frac{3}{4}$-$4\frac{3}{4}$ ins.   C   Dark grey-green. Considerably longer than Bar-Tailed Godwit.
D   In flight broad, white wing-bar, pure white tail with black terminal band, and long legs projecting well beyond tail are distinctive. Taller than Bar-Tailed Godwit when standing. Bill longer and generally straighter. Winter plumage darker brownish-grey than Bar-Tailed Godwit: underparts lighter. In summer plumage both sexes have reddening of plumage, male more than female, but in neither does it extend much lower than upper breast. Lower breast and flanks mainly white with irregular dark barrings. Young are like winter adults, but neck and breast more rufous.
E   Rather silent out of breeding season except for flight call—" wicka . . . wicka . . . wicka "—loud and clear. In breeding-haunts " kwee-yit " call reminiscent of Lapwing, and variety of other notes, notably " grütto . . . grütto . . . grütto " song during display flight.
F   In display flight male rises steeply with rapid wing-beats and trisyllabic note. At about 200 ft. call changes to " grütto . . . grütto . . . grütto," wing-beats are slower, wings bent downwards, tail twisted from side to side as bird " rolls " through air. Song and " roll " cease as bird glides with rigid wings, and, in series of side-slips, comes to earth. " Ceremonial-scraping " on ground.
G   Insects, earthworms, crustacea, mollusca, etc., and some vegetable matter.
H   Typical race breeds in Palæarctic Europe—S. Sweden, S. Baltic islands; sparingly in France, Belgium and Holland. Also Denmark, N. Germany and through Poland, W. Russia into Siberia. Replaced by allied race in E. Siberia, Mongolia, etc. *British Isles:* A century ago bred in fenland and marshes in E. and S. England. Recent sporadic efforts at breeding suggest westward extension of present breeding range. Otherwise regular visitor all months in increasing numbers. Frequent inland.
J   Typical race migrates through Europe and W. Asia to Mediterranean and Africa (to Sudan, Abyssinia and Kenya). In Asia, to Indian Ocean. Eastern race migrates through E. Asia to Philippines, Borneo and N. Australia. *British Isles:* Occurs all months, but chiefly on passage, mainly S. coast, April-May and July-September. Increasing numbers winter here, especially on S.W. coast.
K   Salt marsh and estuarine borders, also mud flats. Frequently inland at sewage farms, fresh-water marshes, etc.
L   Reclaimed grasslands bordering fens and bogs. Occasionally heaths and sand-dunes.
M   Usually a hollow in luxuriant grass lined with a pad of dead grass.   N   Normally 4. Not as glossy as Bar-Tailed Godwit's. Variable ground-colour with umber blotches. Size. c. $2\frac{1}{5}$ by $1\frac{1}{2}$ins.
    O   By both sexes. 24 days.

CURLEW *Numenius arquata arquata* (*Linnæus*, 1758)

A   Variable: 19-25 ins. Generally 22-23 ins.   B   Very long, down-curved. c. 4-6 ins. Dark horn-coloured.   C   Greenish-grey.
D   Largest of our waders. Streaked brown plumage and long, down-curved bill distinctive. Only bird that may be confused with Curlew is Whimbrel, which is 5 ins. shorter, has bill noticeably shorter in comparison, and pale stripes on crown. Whimbrel's " titterel " note is quite dissimilar to Curlew's note. In summer Curlews have darker plumage than in winter. Northern birds have reddish tinge.
E   Commonest note is loud, musical " quoi . . . quoi." Song (not confined to breeding-haunts) begins with low, drawn-out liquid notes. Tempo quickens to louder, high-pitched bubbling trill, sinking again to low notes. Other cries, yelps and squawks on breeding-grounds.

F   Glorious song flight by male who rises, flying low, and suddenly mounts upward with rapidly beating wings. He checks, hangs poised on quivering wings or sinks to ground chanting ecstatically. In nuptial flights pair glide side by side on bowed wings. Pursuit of females by males on ground with great variety of ceremonial—" leap-frogging," bowing, wing-beating, etc.

G   Varies according to habitat. On coast—mollusca, crustacea, fishes, worms and some vegetable matter. Inland—insects, beetles, snails, small frogs, berries, seeds and grain. Gizzard linings regularly evacuated.

H   A widely distributed Palæarctic species, breeding in Europe up to 70° in Norway, Sweden and Finland. Replaced by allied race in E. Siberia. *British Isles:* Resident at all seasons, passage-migrant and winter visitor. Breeds in most counties except S.W. on high ground, but has increased its range latterly, especially in lowland valleys (Trent, Cheshire Plain, etc.).

J   Typical race migrates through mid and S. Europe to Atlantic coast, Mediterranean and African coasts. Continental birds coming to British Isles work down E. and S. coasts and overland, and most cross over to Ireland. *British Isles:* After breeding season many of our residents go W. and S.W. to Ireland for the winter; some cross to Spain. Return migration begins mid-February mainly by W. coast and overland routes. Main body in breeding-haunts by mid-March. Non-breeders seen on shores in summer.

K   Mud flats and saltings, often resorting at high-tide a considerable distance inland to fields and flooded grassland.

L   Chiefly hill-country—heather-moors, peat-mosses and bogs. Increasing tendency to colonise lowland river valleys. Less frequently sand dunes and heaths.

M   Hollow in the ground, 5-5½ ins. across, lined with grasses, heather-twigs, etc., according to locality.
N   Normally 4. Slight gloss and thin shell. Variably drab ground-colour and small blotches. c. 2¾ by 1$\frac{9}{10}$ ins.   O   By both sexes. 28-30 days.

WHIMBREL   *Numenius phæopus phæopus* (*Linnæus*, 1758)

A   c. 15-16 ins.   B   Long and down-curved, but less so than Curlew's. Horn colour. c. 3½ ins.
C   Greenish-grey.

D   c. 5 ins. smaller than Curlew, with relatively shorter bill, has two clear diagnostic features in addition to size. On crown are two broad, dark bands divided by narrower, pale streak. Also an entirely different note—rapid, rippling titter. In flight wing-beats are quicker. Much more approachable than wary Curlew.

E   Rapid tittering—" titti . . . titti . . . titti . . . titti . . . titti . . . tit." Hence local name of " Titterel." " Seven Whistler," another local name, derives from belief that he repeats call seven times. Bubbling song in breeding-haunts.

F   Song flight similar to Curlew's, with bubbling trill not unlike that bird's notes. Males indulge in tumbling flights, or float in circles with down-curved wings. Females also participate.

G   On coasts—small crustacea, mollusca, bivalves, lugworms, etc. Inland—insects, beetles, flies, worms, snails, berries, etc.

H   A Holarctic species. Typical race breeds Iceland, Faeroes, Norway, Sweden, Finland, Estonia, Russia. Allied races in N.E. Asia and N. America. *British Isles:* Summer resident in Orkneys, Shetlands and (occasionally) N. Scotland. Otherwise passage-migrant on all coasts and often inland. Exceptionally in winter. Some non-breeders stay on coasts in summer.

J   Typical race migrates from N. Europe to all coasts of Africa, shores of Indian Ocean and Ceylon. *British Isles:* Summer migrants and considerable number of passage-migrants arrive S. coast mid-April and continue to mid-June. Main arrivals end of April and early May. Return migration begins early July, and continues in strength August and September, diminishing in October. Passage N. by E., W. and overland routes. Passage S. mainly E. coast.

K   Mud flats and saltings, but has fondness for fields and grassland near coast. Occasionally on rocky shores. Infrequent far inland.

L   Northern moorland and heaths amongst heather, cotton-grass and moss. Also heather-covered islands; occasionally rough pastures.

M   Hollow in the grass or heath, usually quite open; lined with moss, heather-twigs, grass, etc.
N   Normally 4. Similar to, but more boldly marked than, Curlew's. c. 2$\frac{3}{10}$ by 1$\frac{3}{5}$ ins.   O   By both sexes. About 24 days.

WOODCOCK *Scolopax rusticola* (*Linnæus*, 1758)

A c. 13½ ins.   B Long, straight and tapering. Dull flesh colour, dark towards tip. c. 3 ins.
C Greenish-flesh.
D Round-winged, somewhat owl-like flight as this medium-sized, russet-coloured bird rises suddenly from cover in open woodland and departs with twisting flight should cause no difficulty in identification. Large bill, much stouter than Snipe's when at rest. Bill often inclined downward in flight. Crepuscular in habit.
E When males are " roding " two cries are heard, a thin " tsiwick," and a low, croaking sound. In courtship twittering note occurs, and there are records of squeaking, rippling and crooning noises at nest.
F Male at dusk and dawn repeatedly traverses circuit on edges of woodland and down woodland rides. This " roding " lasts a quarter of an hour to one hour, and in British Isles may be seen from early March to July. On ground " injury feigning " and adoption of frightening attitude by threatened female has been observed.
G Largely earthworms, but also insects and their larvæ, and some vegetable matter.
H Palæarctic species. Breeds throughout N. Europe to 69½° in Norway and Sweden, to 66½° in Finland, and 66° in N. Russia. Southwards range extends to Pyrenees, Corsica, N. Italy, etc. Also eastwards to Asia Minor and across to Japan, and southwards to Kashmir and Himalayas. *British Isles:* Resident population in most counties. Also winter visitor and passage-migrant.
J N. European birds migrate through Europe, S. to Mediterranean regions and Egypt. Continental immigrants to British Isles mostly from W. Russia, Baltic States, N. Germany, Sweden and Norway. *British Isles:* Arrive E. coast late September to end of November, majority coming in big waves mid-October to mid-November. Many continue westwards to Ireland. Our resident population largely sedentary; some cross to Ireland, and few to Portugal and Spain.
K Open woodland and coverts, especially where there is good cover, and where swampy hollows abound. Dry ground preferred for day-time roosting. Evening flights to marshy ground for feeding purposes. In autumn preference for hill country and moors.
L Habitat does not vary greatly in and out of nesting season, but in nesting season keeps more to cover of woodlands.
M Hollow in mossy ground lined with dead leaves. Often placed close to forest tree or bush.
N Normally 4. Buffish with chestnut and grey spots and blotches. c. 1¾ by 1$\frac{5}{16}$ ins.   O By female only. 20-22 days. Generally double-brooded.

GREAT SNIPE *Capella media* (*Latham*, 1787)

A c. 11 ins.   B Long, straight and tapering. Dark brown with yellowish base. c. 2½ ins.
C Greyish or yellowish-green.
D Considerably larger than Common Snipe. Longer in wing, and much heavier flight. Darker in appearance. In flight shows a conspicuous amount of white on sides of tail. Flight slower and more direct, without twistings of the Common Snipe. Generally alights at no great distance.
E Usually silent, but sometimes emits a guttural croak on rising. In breeding-grounds male has remarkable song—" Bip, bip, bip, bip, bipipere, bipirere," and great variety of piping, warbling, grunting and hissing notes.
F Collective display at special spots in the northern marshes. Males arrive at dusk and spar with each other in simulated battle of formalised character, but chiefly sing in chorus, chatter their bills and display with ruffed feathers, spread wings and fanned tails. Females appear at midnight, are displayed to in increasing frenzy of excitement until dawn, when each flies off with male.
G Chiefly earthworms, snails and slugs: also insects and occasional vegetable matter.
H Bird of the middle Palæarctic region, not in extreme west or east. Breeds in Europe in Norway, Sweden, Finland, Russia and eastwards in Asia to Yenisei. *British Isles:* Very sparse passage-migrant.
J Migration of N. European birds to Mediterranean region, and E. Africa south to Natal and Cape. *British Isles:* Probably few each autumn in E. and S. England. (August to mid-November.) Very rarely winter and spring.
K Rough pastures on more or less dry ground—fields, moorlands, sand dunes, bracken-covered hill slopes, etc., though also marshes.
L Marshes, swamps and morasses. Also moist meadows, or birch and willow scrub. In Norway typically in birch zone on fells.
M Depression in the ground with grass or moss lining. Generally on marshy flats with dense vegetation.
N Normally 4. Buff, boldly blotched with deep brown and grey. c. 1⅞ by 1⅕ ins.   O By female only, apparently. 22-24 days.

COMMON SNIPE *Capella gallinago gallinago* (*Linnæus*, 1758)

A c. 10½ ins.   B Long, straight and tapering. Reddish-brown, darkening at tip. c. 2½ ins.
C Dull, pale greenish.
D As it rises from marshy ground with hoarse " scaap " and zig-zags rapidly away, with its long straight bill and darkly patterned plumage it could only be confused with its two near relatives, the very scarce Great Snipe (longer wings, heavier, direct flight, and conspicuous white on sides of tail) or the Jack Snipe (smaller body, relatively shorter bill, solitary, silent and pitches shortly). Melanistic variety (Sabine's Snipe) is now recognised as dark variety of Common Snipe.
E Hoarse " scaap " as it flies away. In breeding-haunts an agitated " chipper . . . chipper . . . chipper " note. Subdued conversational twittering when feeding in company.
F Display flight, rises with rapidly vibrating wings to a considerable height in great circling flight. At regular intervals wings are laid out flat, body is tilted, and tail feathers are opened out as, curving outwards and slipping downwards, it descends at a tangent. Descent accompanied by resonant, tremulous " drumming " sound. On ground drooped wing and spread tail display.
G Mostly worms: also insects, snails and vegetable matter.
H Holarctic species, breeding across Europe north to 70°, and across Asia to Himalayas. Allied races separated in Iceland, Faeroes, N.E. Asia, N. America and Africa. *British Isles:* Resident, passage-migrant and winter visitor. Breeds locally in suitable localities throughout country. Abundant on passage and in winter.
J Typical form migrates S. through Mediterranean regions to Africa. *British Isles:* Most residents are sedentary in disposition. Some migrate to Ireland. No evidence of British-hatched birds abroad. Passage-migrants arrive from N.W. European countries by E. coast and overland routes. Emigration from S. coast 2nd week October and onwards. Return migration—end of March to end of April. Residents in breeding quarters by mid-March.
K Bogs, swamps, marshes, flooded fields, peat-mosses, sewage farms, etc.
L As above.
M Grass-lined hollow in tussock usually in fairly damp site.   N Normally 4. Olive-grey and brown, boldly blotched with brown, often in zone at larger end. c. 1½ by 1⅕ ins.   O By female only. 19½-20 days. Sometimes double-brooded.

JACK SNIPE *Lymnocryptes minimus* (*Brünnich*, 1764)

A c. 7½ ins.   B Fairly long, straight and tapering. Pale yellow-flesh with black tip. c. 1⅝ ins.
C Greenish.
D Noticeably smaller than Common Snipe with relatively shorter bill. Rises silently, with rather slower flight and less abrupt zig-zagging. Generally pitches again at short distance. Solitary in disposition, but not invariably so. Crown pattern lacks Common Snipe's central stripe. Plumage has more metallic gloss. Tail uniformly dark, lacking Common Snipe's white tips to outer tail feathers.
E Normally silent when flushed. Sometimes may utter low, weak call. In breeding-haunts curious " song," presumably vocal, delivered in air mainly, but also on ground—" Lok . . . toggi, lok . . . toggi, lok . . . toggi, lok . . . toggi."
F Distinctive " song " accompanies display flight as bird planes about. At same time whirring noise similar to Common Snipe's " drumming " is heard. Checking speed, it moves slowly and silently forward, then again violently vibrates wings as it mounts to repeat performance.
G Mainly earthworms: mollusca, insects and vegetable matter incidental.
H A N. Palæarctic species. Breeds N. to 69½° in Norway, N. Sweden, Finland, and N. Russia. *British Isles:* Passage-migrant and winter visitor. Widely distributed, but local and never very numerous. Occasional in summer, but has never been proved to breed.
J Migrates from breeding-grounds to N. Africa (Morocco to Egypt) and south to Blue Nile, Kenya, etc. Also to Iraq, Persia, India, Ceylon and further east. *British Isles:* Passage-migrants and winter visitors arrive E. coast September to November. Peak mid-October to mid-November. Many cross to Ireland. Return migration late March to end of April.
K Much as Common Snipe—bogs, marshy fields and swamps, sewage farms, etc.
L Swamps and bogs of high north. Delights in waterlogged expanses of sedge and cotton-grass.
M Moss-lined scrape in low tussock in a bog.   N Normally 4. Very large for bird's size. Decidedly darker than Common Snipe. c. 1₁₂⁵ × 1⅕ ins.   O Apparently by hen only. 24 days at least.

GREY PHALAROPE *Phalaropus fulicarius (Linnæus,* 1758)

A   c. 8 ins.   B   Short, broad, flattened. Chrome-yellow. c. $\frac{4}{5}$ in.   C   Horn-coloured. Partially webbed feet.

D   Grey and Red-Necked Phalaropes are only British waders that habitually swim on water. In winter, Grey Phalarope has grey and white plumage with dark patch in front of eye and over the cheeks. Has a peculiarly long-bodied appearance. Shorter, broader, mainly yellow bill and more uniform grey back distinguish it from Red-Necked Phalarope. In summer, chestnut underparts, whitish sides of face, and dark brown back streaked with chestnut-buff makes it unmistakable. Conspicuously tame.

E   Low monosyllable of whistling quality—" twit." Flocks keep up low twittering.

F   Meagre data, but probably similar to Red-Necked Phalarope's, female completely dominating male and taking initiative. " Injury-feigning " by male when flushed from eggs.

G   Insects and larvæ, crustacea, mollusca and some vegetable matter, mainly taken from surface of water.

H   N. Holarctic species, breeding Iceland, Spitzbergen, Bear Islands, Novaya Zembla, N. Siberia, New Siberian Islands and N. American arctic islands. *British Isles:* Passage-migrant, most frequently S.W., S. and E. coasts of England. Occasional (storm-driven) inland; chiefly after heavy S.W. gales.

J   Winters S. Atlantic, off coast of Africa; E. coast of S. America to Falkland Islands, and W. coast from S. California to Chile. Accidental India, China, Hawaii, New Zealand. *British Isles:* Passage-migrant early September to early November, though occasional all winter months. Very scarce in spring.

K   Mainly pelagic, frequenting off-shore waters: occasional inland on lakes, etc., usually when storm-driven.

L   Vicinity of tundra pools in high north.

M   Mere depression, scantily lined, on ridge of tundra near fresh-water pools: usually in small colonies.

N   Normally 4. Buffish, boldly blotched and spotted. c. 1$\frac{1}{5}$ by $\frac{4}{5}$ ins.   O   By male alone. Not definitely known—at least 19 days. Single-brooded.

RED-NECKED PHALAROPE *Phalaropus lobatus (Linnæus,* 1758)

A   c. 7 ins.   B   Slender, needle-like. Blackish. c. $\frac{9}{10}$ inch.   C   Dark blue-grey: webs yellowish.

D   Habitually swims. Distinguished from Grey Phalarope in winter by longer and noticeably more slender bill, and by less uniform, darker grey back with whitish streakings. Remarkably tame. In summer has black bill, slate-grey head and upper parts, white throat and underparts, and orange patch on sides of neck. Male duller and smaller than female.

E   Subdued " twit." Variety of other quiet notes in breeding-haunts.

F   Female takes incentive in courtship. She flies short distance " in ceremonial manner," alights, swims in stiff attitude towards male with head lowered, displays, rising erect in water with rapid wing beats. Male responds with " wing-rattling," rises in air and alights on her as she lies on water. After pairing they proceed to "scrape," with " grass-throwing," etc.

G   Mainly insects and larvæ pecked from surface of water, or stirred up to surface by bird spinning round in shallows.

H   N. Holarctic in range, breeding Iceland, Faeroes and northern islands and marshes of Norway, Sweden, Finland, former Baltic States, and Russia. Also in Asia across Siberia, in N. America from Alaska to Greenland. *British Isles:* Summer resident in limited numbers in Orkneys, Shetlands, O. Hebrides, Tiree and co. Mayo. Elsewhere rare passage-migrant. Rare inland.

J   Migrates through Europe to W. Africa, and in Asia to Indian Ocean, in Pacific to Japan and China, through North to Central America. *British Isles:* Rare passage-migrant (September-October); few November, rarely July, August, December. Occasionally spring.

K   Pelagic, but occurs on passage on inland lakes.

L   Wet, grassy bogs with scattered lagoons; tundra marshes.

M   Hollow in tussock, scantily lined. Nests in colonies.   N   Normally 4. Slightly more gloss than Grey Phalarope. Buff ground colour, boldly blotched. c. 1$\frac{1}{5}$ by $\frac{4}{5}$ ins.   O   By male alone. About 20 days. Probably single-brooded.

KNOT *Calidris canutus canutus* (*Linnæus*, 1758)

A   c. 10 ins.   B   Black. c. 1⅜ ins.   C   Olive-green.
D   Considerably larger than Dunlin, of stocky build, in grey-and-white plumage of winter. Knot feeds and rests in densely packed masses. Mass flights, like clouds of smoke constantly changing shape. In flight grey bird with a white wing-bar. Bright rufous underparts in summer dress.
E   Low, monosyllabic " knot," and mellow whistling flight note " quick-ick." Melodious fluty song and other calls on breeding-grounds.
F   Song flight on breeding-grounds in high north—male rises with rapid wing strokes to great height, circles on quivering wings, slowly sinks with stiff wings, and mounts again, then sudden nose-dive with rigid wings. " Injury-feigning."
G   Sandhoppers, small crabs, worms, insects, mollusca, etc. On breeding-grounds some vegetable matter (buds, seeds, algæ).
H   N. Holarctic species breeding in the high north.—Taimyr Peninsula eastwards to New Siberian Islands. Replaced by allied races in Greenland and Arctic America. *British Isles:* Passage-migrant and winter visitor. Abundant E. and W. coasts (Solway to Dee). Few non-breeding birds stay in the summer.
J   Typical race migrates to Mediterranean regions, Black Sea, West Coast Africa, Persia, Ceylon, etc. E. Siberian birds apparently migrate to Australia and New Zealand. *British Isles:* Passage-migrants on move mid-March to early June. Majority pass in May. Southward flow begins end of July and continues to end of November. Largest number second half of August and September, but large waves in October and early November.
K   Prefers extensive coastal and estuarine sand and mud flats. Rare inland.
L   Arctic fells and high plateaux on barren stony ground.
M   Hollow with thick lining of lichens.   N   Normally 4. Greyish with many small brown spots and streaks. 1¹⁄₁₀ by 1⅕ ins.   O   By both sexes. Period not clearly known, but estimated 20-25 days. Single-brooded.

TURNSTONE *Arenaria interpres interpres* (*Linnæus*, 1758)

A   c. 9 ins.   B   Black, Rather short, stout and pointed. c. ⅞ inch.   C   Short. Deep orange in adults. Brownish-yellow in juveniles.
D   Noticeably stouter and larger than Dunlin, with mottled, " tortoise-shell " upper parts, broad black or dark pectoral band, short, orange legs, and boldly pied flight-pattern. Broken colour-pattern makes birds hard to distinguish from typical habitat—seaweed-strewn rocky shore. Lozenge-shaped white patch on rump, enclosed by black, shows well in flight. Fond of resting on high rocks and perches. Pugnacious disposition.
E   A metallic " kit-it-it " when flushed. Quarrelsome birds utter deep husky rattle—" quitta . . . quitta . . .quit-it-it "—heard also in breeding-haunts with variations.
F   No real display recorded beyond impetuous, dashing pursuit of female by male, both in air and on ground.
G   Various insects, etc., living amongst tangles of seaweed and under stones which it jerks aside with swift leverings of bill. Also small mussels and limpets.
H   N. Holarctic species. Typical race breeds W. Greenland, Iceland, Spitzbergen and in continental Europe from islands in Baltic northwards. *British Isles:* Winter visitor and passage-migrant widely distributed on all coasts. Non-breeding birds in summer. No authenticated breeding record.
J   Typical race winters European coastline, African coast to Cape and Mediterranean. In Asia to Indian Ocean, Oceania and Australasia. *British Isles:* Winter residents augmented by passage-birds mid-March and April. Northern passage continues to first week of June. Most pass through in May. Southward passage starts by coastal and inland routes end of July-August.
K   Chiefly rocky, pebbly, seaweed-strewn shores—high-tide line, but also on mud flats, and occasionally inland at sewage farms, etc.
L   Often barren, stony ground with sparse vegetation close to shore or on islands.
M   Sites variable, but marked preference for islands. Scantily lined hollow, sometimes under a shelving stone. Social tendency.   N   Normally 4. Greyish-green, irregularly streaked with brown. c. 1½ by 1⅛ ins.   O   By both sexes. Period unknown. Single-brooded.

DUNLIN *Northern: Calidris alpina alpina (Linnæus, 1758)*
Southern: Calidris alpina schinzii (Brehm, 1822)

A   Northern: up to c. 7½ ins. Southern: c. 6¾ ins.   B   Variable: Black straight or very slightly down-curved. Northern: c. 1¼-1⅖ ins. Southern: c. 1-1⅕ ins.   C   Dark olive.

D   As the two races of Dunlin are inseparable in the field they are treated here together. The commonest shore-bird, in winter it has brownish-grey upper parts, greyish breast and fairly long bill. In breeding-plumage (March right through to October in some specimens) black patch on the lower breast is diagnostic. Very gregarious. Massed aerial manœuvres.

E   When flushed, shrill " tüüp." In flocks, feeding or alighting, soft, musical " purre." Song in breeding season rich, purring trill.

F   Massed flight by flocks, showing now dark, now white, in complicated aerial manœuvres. Display flight by male in breeding-haunts—bird rises vertically, hovers, rising and falling, as it trills, and glides down with wings held vertically.

G   Characteristically it feeds on recently exposed mud flats, poking about and extracting mollusca, crustacea, insects, worms, etc., by sight and touch.

H   Southern form breeds British Isles, Holland, Denmark, N. Germany, S. Norway and Sweden, former Baltic States. Replaced by Northern race in arctic Europe and Siberia, and by Greenland and Canadian forms further west. *British Isles:* Resident (Southern) Dunlins are summer residents, but mostly migrate south, and are replaced by Northern Dunlins in winter.

J   Migration of residents from S. coast end of July. Return migration early March-May. Northern form overlaps at both seasons, but many winter here. Southern Dunlins migrate to N. Africa and Mediterranean. Northern Dunlins have a more extensive range in winter—S. Africa and India. In winter, in effect, we exchange our breeding population of Southern Dunlins for winter resident population of Northern Dunlins. Normal coastal and inland routes at both seasons.

K   All types of muddy, sandy, shingly shores, but typically estuarine flats and creeks. Frequent visitor to inland reservoirs, sewage farms, etc.

L   Typically, elevated moorlands with peaty pools. Also lowland mosses and salt-marshes.

M   Neat cup in a tussock, lined with grass and bents. Often near to water.   N   Normally 4. Slight gloss: thin shell. Variable buffish ground, with brown spots and blotches. c. 1⅖ by 1 ins.   O   By both sexes. 21-22 days. Single-brooded.

CURLEW-SANDPIPER *Calidris testacea (Pallas, 1764)*

A   c. 7½ ins.   B   Slightly down-curved, longish and thin. Blackish-green. Size variable. c. 1⅜ ins.   C   Greenish-brown.

D   Easily overlooked amongst Dunlin. Decurved bill not sufficiently different from variable Dunlin bills to be characteristic. Diagnostic feature is white rump. General effect of upper parts more spotted and mottled. Distinctly longer legs, slender carriage and upright stance. Distinct note. In summer plumage russet underparts. No black as in Dunlin.

E   Distinctive, musical " chirrup." On breeding-grounds alarm note is " wick . . . wick . . . wick." Rattling note during display.

F   Careers about in little flocks on breeding-grounds. Male chases female and glides above her with shivering wings. Other displays not adequately recorded.

G   Similar to Dunlin.

H   N.E. Palæarctic region (E. Arctic Asia) from Gyda and mouth of Yenisei eastward to New Siberian Islands, Kolyma delta and Bering Island. *British Isles:* Passage-migrant in variable strength, chiefly E. and S. coasts. Few winter records, and very few seen inland.

J   Migrates through Europe and Asia to Mediterranean, Africa, Madagascar, etc.; also to Iraq, India, Malaya and Australasia. *British Isles:* Passage-migrants arrive E. coast mid-July to mid-October. Largest numbers in September. Return passage April-June, less regular and numbers much smaller.

K   Mud flats and creeks. Occasionally only, inland, mostly in N. England of birds in autumn crossing to W. coast.

L   Southerly slopes of tundras of the high north, and low-lying ground near rivers.

M   Depression in a little tussock with scanty lining of lichens.   N   Normally 4. Greenish, boldly blotched with red-brown. c. 1⅖ by 1 ins.   O   By both sexes. Period unknown. Single-brooded.

LITTLE STINT *Calidris minuta* (*Leisler*, 1812)

A   c. 5¾ ins.   B Black. c. $\frac{7}{10}$ in.   C Black.

D   Little Stint and Temminck's Stint are our most diminutive waders—at least an inch smaller than Dunlin. Bill short and straight. In winter very white breast and grey upper parts. In summer, upper parts rufous, mottled with black. For differences between this species and Temminck's Stint see under latter. Generally singly or in small parties with Dunlin, etc.

E   When flushed a monosyllabic " chit . . . chit . . . chit." Twittering note amongst feeding flock. Breeding trill—" dirr . . . dirr . . . dirrit " and variants.

F   Ground display with whirring wings before pairing, and " butterfly " hovering flight.

G   Insects—shrimps, sandhoppers, mollusca, worms, etc., and some vegetable matter in breeding-haunts.

H   N. Palæarctic species breeding from northern fringe of N. European coastline and eastward to New Siberian Islands. *British Isles:* Passage-migrant in fluctuating numbers, more commonly in autumn than in spring, and chiefly on E. and S. coasts.

J   Migrates south to Mediterranean, Africa (to Cape), Indian Ocean, Arabia and Ceylon. *British Isles:* Passage-migrants arrive E. coast mid-August to October, with stragglers later. Some cross overland and work down W. coast. Return passage in smaller numbers, most in May.

K   Mud flats and creeks. Occasionally inland.

L   Grassy marshes of high north: also drier tundra and fells.

M   Small cup-shaped depression, well lined with dead leaves of willow, etc.   N Normally 4. Stone, boldly marked with rich brown. c. 1⅛ by ⅘ in.   O By both sexes. Period unknown. Single-brooded.

TEMMINCK'S STINT *Calidris temminckii* (*Leisler*, 1812)

A   c. 5½ ins.   B Very dark brown. c. $\frac{7}{10}$ in.   C Yellowish or greenish brown.

D   In winter this diminutive wader is much greyer than Little Stint, with more uniform colouring, and greyish, not whitish breast, and white outer tail feathers. Little Stint is " Dunlin-like." Temminck's Stint is " Sandpiper-like." In summer the plumage is darker and less rufous than Little Stint's. Primarily fresh-water species—muddy marshes, sewage farms, etc.—whereas Little Stint prefers open shores. When on coast, resorts to muddy creeks and gutters. Tends to tower when flushed.

E   When flushed, high-pitched trilling titter, as opposed to monosyllabic " tit . . . tit . . . tit " of Little Stint. In breeding-haunts tinkling trill, rising and falling, and sustained.

F   Moth-like display flight—wings half raised and quickly vibrated as bird hovers and circles with spread tail. " Injury-feigning " at nest.

G   Chiefly small insects, mollusca, crustacea and worms.

H   N. Palæarctic species, breeding N. and central Norway, N. Sweden, Finland and Russia, across to Siberia (Tchutchki Peninsula). *British Isles:* Has nested in Scotland twice recently, but otherwise irregular and scarce passage-migrant.

J   Migrates south to Mediterranean region, to equatorial Africa; also S. Asia, Arabia, Iraq, India, Ceylon, Malay, China, Japan, etc. *British Isles:* Rare and irregular passage-migrant, end of July to October, mostly in September. Most frequent from Norfolk southwards and along S. coast. Return migration—May and early June.

K   Fresh-water marshes, etc., or, on the coast, in creeks and gutters.

L   Scanty scrub bordering lakes and streams, or in grass-fields near to human habitations.

M   Hollow in the grass, lined with grasses and bents.   N Normally 4. Brownish-buff, evenly spotted with brown. c. 1⅛ by ⅘ ins.   O By both sexes. Period unknown. Single-brooded.

SANDERLING *Crocethia alba (Pallas, 1764)*

A   c. 8 ins.   B   Fairly short. Black. c. 1 in.   C   Black.

D   Plump little wader, slightly larger than Dunlin, extremely active. Delights to feed along tide-edge, retreating from and pursuing breaking waves. In winter—markedly light appearance, breast pearly-white, upper parts very pale grey. Prominent white wing-bar in flight. In summer, upper parts are light chestnut mottled with black, contrasting with pure white belly.

E   Liquid "twick...twick" with twittering from feeding flock. On breeding-grounds male has a strident churring song.

F   Male rises short distance with vibrating wings and makes steep downward flight uttering churring song. Sexual chases and ground display with fluffed-out breast, etc. "Injury-feigning."

G   Small crustacea, mollusca, etc., snatched from receding waves. Vegetable matter freely taken on breeding-grounds.

H   N. Holarctic species, breeding in remote high north—arctic islands of Canada, N. Greenland, Spitzbergen and arctic islands off Siberia. *British Isles:* Passage-migrant and winter visitor, widely distributed on sandy coasts. Chiefly autumn passage, though many winter; a few non-breeding birds stay in summer.

J   European and Asiatic migration to S. Africa, Indian Ocean and Australasia. American migration to winter quarters south U.S.A. to Patagonia. *British Isles:* Arrive mid-July onwards. Adults predominate at first. Two main E. and W. coast streams, E. stream dividing at Lowlands and some cross overland to W. coast. Return migration end of April to mid-June, most birds by W. coast route.

K   Strictly coastal—sandy flats. Exceptional inland.

L   Barren, stony, arctic tundra, with sparse vegetation, generally not many miles from coast.

M   Neat hollow in ground nearly filled with leaves of willow, etc.   N   Normally 4. Olive, sparsely mottled with brown at larger end. c. $1\frac{3}{8}$ by $\frac{9}{10}$ in.   O   By both sexes but principally female. 23-24 days. Single-brooded.

RUFF *Philomachus pugnax (Linnæus, 1758)*

A   Ruff: c. 11-12 ins. Reeve: c. $8\frac{1}{2}$-10 ins.   B   Comparatively short and straight. Black-brown in winter. Variation in summer of yellow, red and orange shades. c. $1\frac{1}{2}$ ins.   C   Colour variable—shades of green, yellow, orange and flesh.

D   In summer extraordinary and variable ruff and eartufts of male are unique. Out of breeding-plumage males and females lack distinctive features and can be puzzling. Differs from Redshank in—shorter bill, rather shorter legs, narrower wing-bar in flight. Oval white patch on each side of dark central area of tail. Most birds seen in Britain are juveniles in autumn plumage—smaller than adults, and showing a neat, bold pattern on back of black, brown feathers, with sharply defined buff borders. Forehead and sides buffish.

E   Very silent bird. Seldom calls when flushed. Variety of hoarse, low, guttural notes in breeding-haunts. Contact-note in flight on migration similar to but quite distinct from Redshank's.

F   Males congregate on "display-grounds," each male on its own stand. There they go through infinite variety of contortions. Birds scuttle about with expanded "ruffs," and spread and flutter their wings. Frequent halts and crouchings, bill to ground, with spasmodic shiverings and spreading of tails. Sham fights frequent. Apparently indifferent females present themselves to mates. Relations promiscuous.

G   Insects, worms, crustacea, mollusca, seeds, etc.

H   Palæarctic species. Breeds W. France, Holland, N. Germany, Denmark, Scandinavia, and central Europe across to Siberia. *British Isles:* Formerly bred regularly in suitable fenland localities, especially Lincs and Norfolk. Now quite exceptional as breeding-species, but occurs as passage-migrant, coasts and inland, mainly in autumn.

J   European breeding birds migrate to Africa (to Cape). In Asia—to Iraq, Persia, India, China, Japan, Borneo, etc. Casual in N. America. *British Isles:* Passage mainly E. coast mid-July to mid-September, mostly August. Most early arrivals come S. of Wash. Very few on W. coast. Return migration April-May mainly by E. coast and inland routes.

K   Swampy ground, flooded meadows, sewage farms, etc. Less regularly estuarine creeks and gutters.

L   Fens and grassy marshes.

M   Hollow, completely hidden, in lush marsh-meadow grass. Lined with a few grasses.

N   Normally 4. Glossy, grey-green, boldly spotted and blotched at thick end. c. $1\frac{3}{4}$ by $1\frac{1}{4}$ in.

O   By female alone. 21 days. Single-brooded.

PURPLE SANDPIPER *Calidris maritima maritima (Brünnich,* 1764)

A c. 8¼ ins.   B Brown-black: base yellow. c. 1 1/10 in.   C Yellowish.

D Chiefly encountered on seaweed-strewn, limpet-covered rocks at foot of cliffs, and on rocky shores and islets. Robust, portly, has a generally sooty appearance relieved by dull, yellowish legs. In summer, feathers on back have rufous edgings, throat and breast strongly streaked and spotted. White wing-bar very noticeable in flight. Very tame and approachable. Swims readily. Commonly in small parties.

E Rather silent bird. Subdued " wit . . . wit " on rising. On breeding-grounds liquid " too . . . it " when flushed.

F Ground display: " wing-ceremony," raising one or both wings vertically whilst standing or running. Display flight with glides on motionless wings. Rat-like " injury-feigning " retreat from nest.

G In winter quarters—insects, crustacea, mollusca, small fish, etc. In breeding-haunts—mainly vegetable—berries, leaves, seeds, etc.

H N. Holarctic. Breeds from arctic Canada eastwards to Siberia (Taimyr Peninsula). *British Isles:* Passage-migrant and winter visitor, widely distributed on rocky shores. A few stay summer. No authenticated breeding recorded, but suspected.

J Winters in Europe—N. Sea and Baltic coasts, seldom straying as far south as the Mediterranean. *British Isles:* Winter visitors and passage-migrants arrive N. half of E. coast, end of July to October. Largest numbers in October. Gradual spread S. and W. (some take W. route). Return migration mid-March to May.

K Coastal species, frequenting rocky, seaweed-strewn shores and islets. Very seldom inland.

L Arctic tundra and fells—bare ridges and summits at south of its range, but nearer coast in far north.

M Neat hole in peat, partly filled with dead leaves of willow, etc.   N Normally 4. Greenish, blotched with brown streaks and hair lines. c. 1½ by 1 in.   O Chiefly by male. 21-22 days. Single-brooded.

COMMON SANDPIPER *Actitis hypoleucos (Linnæus,* 1758)

A c. 7¾ ins.   B Short, straight. Dark-brown. c. 9/10 in.   C Light greenish-grey.

D Small sandpiper with brownish-grey upper parts, pure white belly and well-defined white wing-bar. When disturbed flies off low over water with shrill " twee . . . wee . . . wee " and spasmodic wing-action. Frequenter of hill-streams and lakes. Mostly found inland. For differences between Green and Wood Sandpipers see under those species.

E Characteristic shrill, " twee . . . wee . . . wee " repeated in quick succession three or more times. Display song, " kittiweewit . . . kittiweewit . . . kittiweewit."

F Variable. Male flies rapidly round in circles uttering song, or both sexes indulge in zig-zagging, swerving flight, male pursuing with slow, bat-like flight. Ground chase, male pursuing female with wing or wings raised and tail fanned. Injury-feigning frequent.

G Chiefly insects—mayflies, beetles, caddis-flies, etc., also worms, small mollusca, crustacea, etc.

H Palæarctic. Breeds from southern to arctic (mainland) Europe. Also recorded nesting in Africa. *British Isles:* Summer resident in most counties except S.E. Chiefly confined to hilly districts with rushing streams. As passage-migrant widely distributed all coasts and inland.

J Winters throughout Africa, and in S. Arabia, India, China, Australia and Tasmania. *British Isles:* Contrary to usual custom of waders it uses W. coast more than E. coast routes. Inland waters much frequented, especially on W. side of England. Northward passage mid-April to end of May. Southward passage, mid-July to September, mostly in late August.

K Prefers running to still waters, and frequents lowland streams and lakes in preference to marshes. Regularly in coastal drains and gutters in autumn, but seldom on open shores.

L Hill streams and lakes: borders of lochs and tarns.

M On or near banks of streams or lochs, often on a slope, with some sheltering vegetation. Scanty lining of bents, etc.   N Normally 4. Buffish, with dark chestnut markings. c. 1½ by 1 in.

O By both sexes. 21-23 days. Single-brooded.

WOOD SANDPIPER *Tringa glareola* (*Linnæus*, 1758)

A c. 8 ins.   B Short. Black-brown, base greenish. c. 1⅛ in.   C Yellowish-green.
D Rather larger and much longer-legged than Common Sandpiper; rather smaller and lighter-hued than Green Sandpiper. At all seasons it lacks the bold black and white of the Green Sandpiper in flight. The undersides of its wings are light greyish—not dark. White rump is conspicuous but not markedly so. In summer plumage the back is conspicuously mottled and chequered with whitish markings. Feet project beyond the tail in flight. Distinctive note when flushed.
E An excited " chiff-chiff-chiff," shriller and less musical than Green Sandpiper's note. Two types of song in breeding-haunts, yodelling song with woodlark quality notes, and also peculiar drumming note.
F Display flight, slow wing-beats changing to tremulous flutter as bird rises, then with set wings down-curved, it mounts a little further under initial impetus, and then glides down with spread tail and wings, singing as it does so. Ground display of " leap-frogging " type.
G Chiefly insects, spiders, worms, etc.
H N. Palæarctic species—commonest sandpiper of the northern forest belt. Breeds from N. Scandinavia, Finland, and Russia, south to Belgium and Holland. *British Isles:* Passage-migrant mainly E. and S.E. coasts and inland waters not far from coast. Bred Northumberland 1853.
J Migrates through Europe to Africa, S. Asia and Australia. Does not winter north of Mediterranean. *British Isles:* Passage-migrant mainly along southern part of east coast route. Exceptional elsewhere, but generally seen inland not far from coast.
K Marshy and muddy regions on borders of lakes, etc., usually near coast. Occasionally in salt-marshes, but seldom on the open shore.
L Wet swamps and margins of forest pools.
M Usually small hollow in marshy ground. In flooded forest regions the old nests of Fieldfares, etc., used.   N Normally 4. Great variation in colour. Greenish-buff with zoning of bold blotches on larger end. c. 1½ by 1 in.   O By both sexes. Period unknown. Single-brooded.

GREEN SANDPIPER *Tringa ochropus* (*Linnæus*, 1758)

A c. 9 ins.   B Black-brown with dark green base. c. 1³⁄₁₀ in.   C Olive-green.
D Larger, stouter and considerably darker than Common Sandpiper. In flight conspicuously black and white—like a large House Martin. Pure white rump, tail and belly contrast strongly with dark upper parts. Underside of wings blackish (Wood Sandpiper greyish). When flushed rises high and often zig-zags, uttering triple " tweet-weet-weet."
E Full, clear, musical " tweet-weet-weet " when flushed: very distinct from " chiff-chiff-chiff " of Wood Sandpiper, or shrill " twee-wee-wee " of Common Sandpiper. Rippling song during display flight in breeding-haunts.
F Display flight—alternate rising on rapidly vibrating wings, and steep gliding with down-curved wings. Ground display with head lowered, tail spread and raised, and wings drooped. " Leap-frogging," of courting pairs observed.
G Chiefly insects, small worms, mollusca and some vegetable matter.
H Palæarctic species. Breeding distribution coincides with Wood Sandpipers', but extends not so far north and further south. *British Isles:* Has bred in Lake District (1917) and suspected at other times elsewhere. Otherwise, passage-migrant, fairly frequent, autumn and spring. Some winter here.
J Winters in S. Europe and Africa, also south Asia and Malay. *British Isles:* From breeding-grounds arrives E. coast mid-July to end of September, and birds spread inland and pass S. and W. by overland routes. Very frequent at inland lakes, reservoirs, sewage farms, etc. Return passage March and April in smaller numbers.
K Borders of lakes, rivers, streams, ditches, inland where other waders are infrequent. Very faithful to chosen sites. On coast—gutters and drains: rarely open shores.
L Marshy, wooded districts in the vicinity of ponds, forest pools, alder swamps.
M Normally old nest of another bird—Fieldfare, Jay, Woodpigeon, etc., or old Squirrel's drey or clump of pine needles lodged in tree. No lining except moss.   N Normally 4. Greenish or buffish sparingly spotted with brown and grey. c. 1⁷⁄₁₂ by 1⅛ ins.   O Chiefly by female. c. 20 days. Normally single-brooded.

REDSHANK *British: Tringa totanus britannica (Mathews, 1935). Continental: T. t. totanus (Linnæus, 1758). Icelandic: T. t. robusta (Schiöler, 1919)*

A   c. 11 ins.   B   Fairly long, tapering. Pink-horn: base of lower mandible orange-yellow. c. 1½ ins.   C   Adult: Orange-red. Juvenile: pale orange-yellow.

D   Orange-red legs, conspicuous pattern in flight (white rump and tail-coverts, and broad, white crescent on hind border of wing), easily distinguish this noisy, excitable, medium-sized wader. Three forms now separated are indistinguishable in field in winter. In summer continental Redshank is darker above and more streaked. Icelandic Redshank is more so, and slightly larger.

E   All notes have wild, musical quality. Flushed birds utter melodious " tūiū," or triple " tu-hu-hu." Display flight accompanied by yodelling " dhu-lee, dhu-lee, du le, dle, dle, dle." In breeding-haunts many variants and other notes of alarm and excitement.

F   Song flight: bird rises with shivering wings, shoots upwards and sinks with wings bowed downwards, yodelling, wings raised vertically for instant on alighting. Ground display in pairs or small groups, with characteristic pursuit and postures. Tremulously fluttering wings and high-stepping precede coition.

G   Largely insects, mollusca, crustacea, worms and some vegetable matter.

H   Continental form breeds across Europe southwards from Spain and Italy to N. Norway, Finland and Russia. Icelandic form restricted to Iceland and possibly Faeroes. *British Isles:* British form restricted to British Isles: resident, and increasing range W. and S. during last century. Now in all counties except Cornwall and Pembroke. Icelandic and probably some Continental birds winter here, but impossible to differentiate in winter plumage.

J   Continental birds winter W. coast of Europe, Mediterranean, N.W. and N.E. African coasts to Red Sea, Arabia and Malaya. Icelandic birds winter W. coast of Europe, and Africa. *British Isles:* British residents mainly sedentary: others show southward trend and some cross Channel. Nesting areas occupied mid-February to end of March, and coastal movement starts early June-July. Passage-migrants arrive latter half of August to early November on both E. and W. coasts, and return March and April.

K   Tidal estuaries and mud flats. Some linger inland in winter.

L   Grassy marshes and lowland moors on coast and far inland.

M   Generally a well-concealed hollow in a grass tuft, with grass stems twined overhead to give concealment. Lining of dry grasses.   N   Normally 4. Buffish grey with handsome sienna blotches. c. 2 by 1¼ ins.   O   By both sexes. 23-24 days. Single-brooded.

SPOTTED REDSHANK *Tringa erythropus (Pallas, 1764)*

A   c. 12 ins.   B   Fairly long, straight, tapering. Dark-brown: dusky-red at base of lower mandible. c. 2¼ ins.   C   Summer: Very dark red and brown. Winter: Orange-red.

D   In summer alternative name, Dusky Redshank, applies to this species, which then has strikingly black plumage, spotted with white on back. In winter has more ashy-grey appearance, wing-coverts and scapulars spotted with white. Differs from Redshank in distinctly larger size, spotted appearance, and no white wing-bar in flight. Quite distinct note.

E   Easily recognised " chew-it " flight note. On breeding-grounds variant of this note drawn out or quickened in distinctive pattern.

F   No special display yet described, though Redshank " struttings " observed by birds in breeding-plumage on passage.

G   Almost entirely animal matter—insects, mollusca, crustacea, small fishes, small frogs, tadpoles, etc.

H   N. Palæarctic species. Breeds in northern Europe (Scandinavia, Finland, N. Russia) and in Asia (through Siberia to Kamtschatka). *British Isles:* Uncommon passage-migrant in autumn and spring, chiefly Norfolk to Sussex coasts. Occasional inland.

J   Winters in Mediterranean and Black Sea regions, and in S. Asia. *British Isles:* Passage-migrants arrive E. coast mid-July to mid-October. Mostly August and September. Passage mainly down E. coast, and emigration from S. coast E. of Isle of Wight. Small numbers use overland routes. Return passage in small numbers end of April to June.

K   Coastal flats and salt-marshes, and inland marshes, sewage farms, etc.

L   Swamps in forested country: sometimes in open pine forests or dry heather.

M   Scantily lined depression in tussock—sometimes on burnt-out ground.   N   Normally 4. Olive-brown, boldly blotched with umber at the thick end. c. 2 by 1¼ ins.   O   Apparently only by male. Period unknown. Single-brooded.

GREENSHANK *Tringa nebularia* (*Gunnerus*, 1767)

A   c. 12 ins.   B   Slightly upturned. Bluish-slate; tip horn. c. 2-2¼ ins.   C   Pale olive-green.

D   Apart from colour of legs, Greenshank is larger, taller and greyer bird than Redshank. No white on the wing, but lower back, rump and tail are conspicuously white. Bill is slightly upturned. Greenish feet project beyond tail in flight. In winter plumage upper parts are delicate grey; in summer back plumage is much darker and breast boldly spotted with black.

E   When flushed: " tew . . . tew . . . tew," lower in pitch and less musical than Redshank. Excitable " chip-chip-chip " on breeding-grounds, and great variety of other notes. Song, rich, full-toned " tew-hoo, tew-hoo, tew-hoo . . . "

F   Ground display, male bowing to female with much clicking of bills, " leap-frogging " and wing-raising. Ecstatic wing-shivering before coition. Aerial coition observed. Song flight with undulating " switch-back " and tense rhythmic beating of wings, and glides.

G   Almost entirely animal matter—insects, beetles, mollusca, crustacea, tadpoles, frogs, etc.

H   N. Palæarctic species—N. and central Scandinavia, Finland, former Baltic states, N. Russia and in Asia through Siberia and south to Turkestan, etc. *British Isles:* Summer resident in N. Scotland and some outer islands. Passage-migrant all coasts, and frequently inland. Fairly frequent in winter.

J   Widespread wintering movements—to Mediterranean, Africa (to Cape), Black Sea, N. India, China, Japan, Ceylon, Tasmania, New Zealand. *British Isles:* Breeding birds arrive from late March. Migrants, mid-April to early June. Leisurely southwards movement mainly by inland routes late June. Many cross Scotland E. to W. and go to Ireland. Emigration from S. coast August to mid-October.

K   On borders of lakes, rivers, marshes and sewage farms, etc. Also coastal estuaries, but less frequently on open shores.

L   Extensive, tree-less moorlands interspersed with lochs; also heathy tracts in forested country.

M   Hollow, lined with leaves, pine needles, etc., generally near a conspicuous object—bare log, large stone, etc.   N   Normally 4. Buffish with variable markings over whole egg. c. 2 by 1⅜ ins.

O   By both sexes, but chiefly by female. 24-25 days. Single-brooded.

RINGED PLOVER *Charadrius hiaticula hiaticula* (*Linnæus*, 1758)

A   c. 7½ ins.   B   Adult male at all times, and adult female in summer: bright yellow, tip black. Adult female and 1st year juveniles in winter: upper mandible horn-coloured, lower mandible yellow. c. ⅝ in.   C   Summer: both sexes bright yellow. Winter: Adult female and 1st year young: lemon. Juveniles: yellowish-flesh.

D   Small, robust, with conspicuous black collar below white throat and sides. Yellow legs diagnostic (Kentish—black: Little Ringed Plover—pale flesh). In flight well-marked narrow white wing-bar and call note should distinguish from Little Ringed Plover. Also no white band above black forehead. Continuous black chest-band immediately distinguishes it from Kentish Plover, as also yellow legs and bill. (Kentish—black bill and legs). Arctic Ringed Plover, recently separated as sub-species, winters here and has darker upper parts.

E   Liquid, fluty " tooli " on being approached. Great variety of notes when breeding, mostly of softly melodic quality. Flight song " quit . . . u-wit . . . quit . . . u-wit, quit . . . u-whit."

F   Male postures before female in crouching attitude with upraised feathers and depressed tail. Black gorget fluffed out. " Scrape " ceremony. Aggressive posturing of rival males. Courtship flights of both birds with slow wing-beats. Coition unrelated to display. Injury-feigning.

G   Mollusca, crustacea, insects, flies, snails, worms, etc.

H   Holarctic species, widely distributed on coasts and inland rivers. Baffin Island, S. Greenland, Iceland, Faeroes, Britain, non-arctic Scandinavia, shores of Baltic, N. Sea and N. shores of Mediterranean. Arctic sub-species (*C. h. tundræ*) in high arctic—European and Asiatic Siberia. *British Isles:* Resident all coasts, and some breed inland.

J   Northern birds winter on coastline of central and S. Europe, Mediterranean and W. Africa. *British Isles:* Our breeding population are summer residents and only few remain after July, some appear sedentary, but majority work south and migrate to Ireland, France and further south. Many winter on S. coast of England. Arctic race is passage-migrant and winter visitor. Return migration from mid-March and onwards.

K   Sandy and muddy shores: frequently inland when on passage.

L   Sandy and pebbly shores: sometimes in fallow land, amongst growing corn, and on inland wastes and warrens.

M   Scrape in sand or shingle, usually lined with fragments of shell, small stones, etc.   N   Normally 4. Greyish, spotted brown-black. c. 1³⁄₁₀ by 1 ins.   O   By both sexes. 23-26 days. Double-brooded.

KENTISH PLOVER *Leucopolius alexandrinus alexandrinus* (*Linnæus*, 1758)

A   c. 6¼ ins.   B   Black. c. 1⅙ inch.   C   Lead-grey.

D   Smaller and slighter than Ringed Plover: dark patches on side of breast instead of continuous dark band. Other black markings fainter and less extensive. White patch on forehead continues over eye, giving impression that narrow dark band below runs continuously through the eye. In summer, crown is more rufous than black. Female lacks dark mark on forehead, and breast-patches and eye-stripe are dusky brown. Black legs and black bill are diagnostic at all seasons: also 3 white outer pairs of tail feathers.

E   Noisy little bird. Monosyllabic " wit . . . wit . . . wit " and flute-like " piu " are commonest calls. Song—a succession of notes running into a trill, " trit . . . trit - ritritritrirr."

F   Moth-like wavering song flight, with fully extended wings, and body thrown from side to side. Ground display not fully described. Injury-feigning.

G   Insects—beetles, flies, spiders, small snails, worms, sandhoppers, etc.

H   Widely distributed over central and southern Europe and Asia, not breeding as far north as previous two species. *British Isles:* Very few pairs may still nest Kent-Sussex coast; otherwise very rare migrant, spring and autumn, exceptionally in winter.

J   Winters throughout Africa to Cape. Also India and E. to Japan. *British Isles:* A few birds intending to breed may arrive mid-April and stay to late September. Otherwise sparse migrant April-May and August-September on S. and E. coasts. Occasionally inland. Elsewhere rare vagrant.

K   Coastlines and rivers, and open spaces inland.

L   Shingle beds and sandy beaches: abroad, sometimes nests far inland on dried mud in estuaries, etc.

M   Mere hollow scraped in sand, eggs often buried point downwards. Preference for slightly elevated site.

N   Normally 3. Very variable—normally stone-buff with irregular black streaks and dots. c. 1³⁄₂₀ by ⁹⁄₁₀ ins.   O   By both sexes. 24 days. Probably double-brooded.

LITTLE RINGED PLOVER *Charadrius dubius curonicus* (*Gmelin*, 1789)

A   c. 6 ins.   B   Blackish with yellow at base of lower mandible. c. ⁹⁄₁₀ inch.   C   Pale flesh.

D   Much like Ringed Plover, but slighter in build and a little smaller. Absence of white wing-bar diagnostic in flight. Bright yellow orbital ring round the eye conspicuous at close range, also narrow, white band over head above black forehead-band. More fresh-water, inland bird than Ringed Plover. Note distinctive.

E   " Tee-ū," noticeably higher in pitch and thinner in sound than Ringed Plover. Anxiety and other explosive and nasal notes when breeding. Courtship song as Ringed Plover's, but ordinarily not passing into trill.

F   Butterfly-like display flight with long, slow wing-beats. Male on ground has high-stepping approach and puffed-out breast on approaching female. Elaborate " scrape " and " nest-relief " ceremonies with much tossing of little pebbles by both birds.

G   Chiefly insects and their larvæ, beetles, flies, spiders, small mollusca, worms, seeds, etc.

H   Palæarctic and Oriental in distribution, replaced by allied races in India and S. China. Breeds in Europe from France, Belgium and Holland north to S.E. Norway and south to Spain, N.W. Africa, S. Italy, etc. Westward colonising trend observable in recent years, hence: *Great Britain:* odd pairs have nested in S.E. counties since 1938, otherwise very rare vagrant.

J   Northern breeders migrate to just beyond equator in Africa and Asia. *British Isles:* Practically unknown outside S.E. England. Apart from recent breeding records, has occurred less than 20 times.

K   On coast and inland waters with gravelly or shingly edges.

L   Markedly more fresh-water bird than Ringed Plover. Found usually inland on gravel pits, reservoirs, etc., with shingly edges, or on waste ground.

M   Hollow in sand or shingle, with scanty lining of stalks, bits of shell, etc.   N   Normally 4. Bluish-green or buffish with brown streaks and spots. c. 1³⁄₂₀ by ⁹⁄₁₀ ins.   O   By both sexes. 24-25 days. Single-brooded in north, but double-brooded in central and S. Europe.

GOLDEN PLOVER *Southern: Pluvialis apricaria apricaria (Linnæus, 1758)*
Northern: Pluvialis apricaria altifrons (Brehm, 1831)

A   c. 11 ins.   B   Black. c. 1 in.   C   Greenish-grey.

D   At all seasons spangled, black and gold pattern on upper parts. In summer plumage northern and southern forms can be readily distinguished—northern have clean, clear-cut pattern of black and white on head and underparts. Southern birds (our breeding stock) have facial and breast pattern much less clear-cut. Face and throat dusky and mottled. In winter plumage races are indistinguishable. Black disappears and replaced by dusky mottling. To distinguish between Golden and Grey Plover in winter dress—Golden has spangled gold on back, and white axillaries (arm-pits); Grey (larger bird, heavier bill) has grey-brown back and black axillaries.

E   A musical, whistling " tlūi." Alarm-note " tlee-oo." Song, rippling " tōo-rōo, tōo-rōo," uttered in air and on ground. Display flighting accompanied by characteristic " sobbing "—" terr-pee-ōo, terr-pee-ōo."

F   Display flight—slow, clipping flight with erratic bursts, often finishing with " nose-dive." On the ground males have display-centres, where they attack one another with wing flapping and " leap-frogging." Aerial sexual chases. Ceremonial scrape-making. Injury-feigning.

G   Varied: insects, worms, snails, slugs, larvæ, small crustacea, seeds, berries, seaweed, etc.

H   Southern race breeds Great Britain, Holland, Denmark, S. Norway and Sweden, and N. Germany. Northern race breeds Iceland, Faeroes, N. Scandinavia, Finland, N. Russia to Yenisei. *British Isles:* Resident, passage-migrant and winter visitor. Breeds sparingly W. Somerset, Devon and S. Wales. More plentifully N. Wales, Pennines, Lake District and through Scotland and northern islands.

J   Impossible to separate Northern and Southern forms in winter, but Golden Plover (? form) migrate to N. Africa, Arabia and N. India. *British Isles:* Probably most of our breeding-stock in British Isles winters here, dispersing from breeding-quarters early July and onwards. Northern immigrants pass through spring and autumn and some stay. W. coast routes more favoured than E. Few in S.E. England.

K   Pastures and grass-fields, arable, stubble, etc., sometimes on shore, but chiefly in hard weather.

L   Upland moors with short heather and peat bogs.

M   Depression in peat with scanty lining of lichen, heather-twigs, etc.   N   Normally 4. Buffish with bold dark blotches, mostly at thicker end. c. 2 by 1⅜ ins.   O   By both sexes. 27-28 days. Single-brooded.

GREY PLOVER *Squatarola squatarola (Linnæus, 1758)*

A   c. 11 ins.   B   Black. c. 1 inch.   C   Ash-grey.

D   Plumage pattern resembles Golden Plover, but in summer, silver-grey (not gold) spangling on upper parts is distinctive. In winter upper parts are brownish-grey and have a much more uniform appearance than Golden Plover. In flight black axillaries (in arm-pit under wing) are diagnostic. Whitish rump and tail and whitish wing are also distinctive in flight. Grey Plovers rather larger, stouter than Golden Plover, and far more restricted to coastal regions.

E   Flight note similar to but higher-pitched than Golden Plover's " tlūi." More like " tlee-oo-ee." Variants of this on breeding-grounds.

F   Very dashing flight, with plunges reminiscent of Lapwing's. Also " hovering " display, and ground-display with fanned tail and wings, and crouchings. Not thoroughly studied yet.

G   Worms, mollusca, crustacea, insects, beetles and some vegetable matter.

H   Holarctic species breeding on tundras of high north—N. Russia and Siberia and arctic America. *British Isles:* Passage-migrant and winter visitor, chiefly in south. Few non-breeders stay the summer.

J   In winter it ranges coastline of Europe, Asia, Africa, Australia and America. *British Isles:* Southerly passage starts mid-July, N.E. coast of Britain, and continues to mid-November. Mostly mid-August and September. Southerly stream splits in lowlands and some cross to W. coast. Wintering birds less susceptible than most species to weather change. Regular winter flocks in some strength on S. coast. Our winter visitors move north March-April by same passage routes. Largest numbers of migrants pass through in May.

K   Mud flats and estuaries: exceptionally inland.

L   Arctic tundra beyond tree-limit.

M   Depression in mossy peat, scantily lined with mosses and lichens.   N   Normally 4. Ground-colour, variable—buffish, lightly spotted and streaked. c. 2 by 1⅖ ins.   O   By both sexes. ? 23 days. Single-brooded.

DOTTEREL *Eudromias morinellus (Linnæus, 1758)*

A   c. 8½ ins.   B   Short, black. c. ⅝ in.   C   Dull yellow.

D   Same carriage as Golden and Grey Plovers, but markedly smaller, and with dark back, and prominent broad white eye-stripe meeting in nape. Dark breast separated from striking chestnut belly by prominent white band. Winter plumage duller in every way. Exceptionally tame and approachable.

E   Sweet, twittering whistle, " whit-a-wee, wit-a-wee, wit-a-wit," and great variety of sweet, rippling, jangling and explosive notes in breeding-haunts.

F   Much of display centres round scrape, female often taking initiative. Both sexes " scrape " and jerk material over shoulders. Wing stretching and sexual flights of varied character. Elaborate " injury-feigning."

G   Mainly insects and beetles, flies, earthworms. mollusca, berries, etc.

H   N. Palæarctic species, breeding up to 71° in Norway, Sweden, Finland and Russia. Breeds S. to high fells of S. Norway, Sweden and locally in German and Austrian mountains. *British Isles:* Summer resident in decreasing numbers. Westmorland, Cumberland, Cairngorms, Grampians and E. Ross. Otherwise sparse passage-migrant.

J   Migrates through Europe and Asia to N. Africa, Arabia, Sinai, Iraq and Persia. *British Isles:* More commonly seen on spring passage, but impossible to distinguish intending residents and passage-migrants. Arrives S. coast end of April to end of May, and works north by inland routes and near coast.

K   On passage in this country—moors, hill-pastures, occasionally lowland heaths and fallows, coastal marshes and grasslands. In winter quarters—open tracts and semi-desert.

L   Barren mountain-tops and high fells in this country (2,500 ft. and above in England, 3,200-4,000 ft. in Scotland). In arctic—low fells and tundra.

M   Depression in ground, unlined or sparingly lined with mosses, lichens, etc.   N   Normally 3. Clay ground colour, heavily blotched. 1⅝ by 1⅜ ins.   O   By male almost entirely. 21½-25½ days. Single-brooded.

BLACK-WINGED STILT *Himantopus himantopus himantopus (Linnæus, 1758)*

A   c. 15 ins.   B   Long, needle-like, and very slightly upcurved. Black. c. 2⅗ ins.   C   Remarkably long. Winter: rose-red. Summer: vermilion.

D   Enormously long, pink legs; straight, black, needle-like bill, and boldly contrasted black-and-white plumage unmistakable. Flight direct with fairly quick beats of pointed wings, legs held out rigidly behind.

E   A sharp " kik . . . kik . . . kik " with variants.

F   Male dances from one leg to other with body held in curious—almost vertical—position, and wings fanning slowly and rhythmically together. Much straw-throwing by both birds at nest-relief ceremony.

G   Insects and larvæ chiefly picked from surface of water. Also water-snails, tadpoles, worms and some vegetable matter.

H   Almost cosmopolitan. Southern Europe to Asia: south to Africa and Ceylon. Sporadically in recent years in Holland, Belgium, Germany, etc. *British Isles:* Normally rare vagrant, but exceptional number arrived 1945 and 3 pairs nested in Nottinghamshire.

J   Northern nesting birds winter in Africa and S. Asia. *British Isles:* Rare vagrant chiefly April to November—some 30 records only.

K   Shallow lakes and lagoons, flooded marshes, quiet riversides. Hardly ever seen on sea-shore.

L   Weedy, shallow lagoons and flooded areas.

M   Often in tussock surrounded by water; sometimes on dried mud by edge of lagoon.

N   Normally 3-4. Clay with black spots and blotches. c. 1¾ by 1⅕ ins.   O   By both sexes. About 25-26 days. Single-brooded.

AVOCET *Recurvirostra avosetta* (*Linnæus*, 1758)

A   c. 17 ins.   B   Conspicuously upcurved and slender. Black. c. 3¼ ins.   C   Blue-grey.
D   Snow-white plumage relieved by striking pattern of black barrings, and long, upcurved bill, make it unmistakable. In flight, legs extend considerably beyond tail. Might be overlooked by superficial glance when in company of Black-headed Gulls.
E   Ordinary call-note clear " klooit," repeated with variants when alarmed or excited in breeding-haunts.
F   Group display with birds in a circle, heads bowing, and much bill-sweeping, water-pecking, straw-throwing, etc. This leads to fighting mixed with formalised ceremonial behaviour in between. In paired birds ceremonial precedes coition, generally in shallow water. Afterwards pair run side by side with crossed bills, male with half-spread wings.
G   Insects, crustacea, etc., obtained by sweeping movements from shallow water.
H   In Europe breeds locally on coasts of N. Sea and Baltic: also Portugal, Spain, S. France, Mediterranean, Black Caspian, and Aral Seas, also throughout Africa and across Balkans, through Asia to China. *British Isles:* After lapse of century bred Ireland 1938 and E. Anglia 1947 and 1948. Otherwise migrant of sparse but fairly regular occurrence.
J   Northern European birds winter in Africa and S. Asia. *British Isles:* Occurs with some regularity E. and S.E. counties from Norfolk to Sussex and Hants, chiefly end of March to June. Has occurred in all other months and fairly often in winter. Very rare W. coast and N. of Yorks.
K   Muddy coasts at mouth of estuaries and flats bordering large inland lakes.
L   River deltas or brackish lagoons with extensive muddy flats.
M   Usually in colonies. Slight hollow with variable lining in low-lying meadows, sandy flats, or on islands in lagoons.   N   Normally 4. Clay-buff irregularly spotted. c. 2⅕ by 1⅜ ins.   O   By both sexes. 22-24 days. Single-brooded.

LAPWING *Vanellus vanellus* (*Linnæus*, 1758)

A   c. 12 ins.   B   Shortish. Black. c. 1 in.   C   Brownish-flesh.
D   Metallic green upper parts, black crest, black on breast and chestnut under tail are distinctive features. General appearance on ground, black and white. In flight, broad round wings (male, very rounded; female narrower, less rounded) and relatively slow flapping action are characteristic. A gregarious species.
E   " Pee-wit "—unmistakable. Spring-song, " Peer-weet, weet . . . peer . . . weet " accompanies tumbling flight.
F   In display flight male rises with very slow wing-beats, quickens pace, rises abruptly and suddenly plunges down, turning and twisting as though almost out of control, then sweeps off with side-to-side tilting flight, and audible rasp of wings. Ground display centred on " scrape."
G   Worms and insect larvæ (wireworms and crane-fly larvæ), mollusca, etc.; some vegetable matter.
H   Palæarctic species, breeding from edge of Arctic circle down to Mediterranean. *British Isles:* Summer resident, passage-migrant and winter visitor. Generally distributed.
J   Many European birds migrate south to Mediterranean, N. Africa, Palestine, Iraq, India and across to Japan. *British Isles:* Recovery of ringed birds bred here shows that migration is largely individual. Some are sedentary, others disperse locally, three-fifths migrate to France, Spain, Portugal and further S. and E. Flocking begins late June. Southward movement by E. and W. and inland routes. Continental Lapwings arrive here chiefly October from Baltic countries and return February-April.
K   Open spaces with early accessible soil. Predominantly farm-land bird. Sometimes on coast, especially in hard weather.
L   Grassland and arable. Rushy fields and moorlands more favoured than at other times. Breeds on most types of open country, including coastal shingles (uncommon).
M   Several pairs often breed in company. Muddied hollow in the ground, lined with grass stalks, etc.
N   Normally 4. Clayish covered with bold black spots and blotches. c. 1⅞ by 1³⁄₁₀ in.   O   By both sexes. 24-27 days. Single-brooded.

OYSTER-CATCHER *Hæmatopus ostralegus* (*Linnæus*, 1758)

A c. 17 ins.   B Long, stout, orange-red. c. 3 ins.   C Winter: flesh-pink. Summer: coral-pink. Juvenile: 1st winter—pale-pink.

D Boldly pied plumage, long orange-red bill and pinkish legs easily distinguish Oyster-Catcher. Strikingly pied pattern in flight. In winter, front and sides of neck white. British (*H. o. occidentalis*), Continental (*H. o. ostralegus*), Icelandic (*H. o. malacophaga*) [dubious], S. and E. Russian (*H. o. longipes*) and E. Siberian (*H. o. osculans*) forms have been separated. Indistinguishable in field.

E Shrill, clear " kleep, kleep " with variants. " Piping performance " song is succession of " kleep " notes, sinking and gathering speed into wavering trill.

F " Piping performance " of two or more birds—often parties up to dozen—continued long after breeding season. With neck thrust forward, shoulders elevated, bills down-pointing, birds run around in curves or spin round on same spot, frantically piping. " Butterfly-flight " by male also occurs.

G Chiefly mussels, limpets, cockles: also crustacea, insects, etc.

H Cosmopolitan in range in different geographical forms. Breeds Iceland, Faeroes, coasts of N. Europe and Baltic, south to Spain, Carmargue, Italy, Macedonia. Also Asia Minor, Black and Caspian Seas. *British Isles:* Resident passage-migrant and winter visitor. Increasing breeding range inland, up river valleys. Otherwise coastal. Breeds all round coasts of British Isles where conditions favourable.

J Winters on European coastline, and S. to Mediterranean and Red Seas, and African coast. *British Isles:* Southwards dispersal after breeding season, mid-July to end of August in British Isles. Most winter on E. and W. coasts from Tay and Clyde southwards, sometimes in enormous numbers. Impossible to differentiate between movements of British breeders and continental immigrants. Return-breeding to sites in spring begins early February, but mainly early March to mid-April.

K All types of sea-coast, but estuaries largely favoured. Infrequent on inland waters.

L On or near shore—shingle beds, sand dunes, grassy flats, headlands, etc. In N. England and Scotland birds follow rivers and streams often far inland.

M Shallow depression lined with small stones and shells.   N Normally 3. Stone-buff with brown-black streaks and blotches. c. $2\frac{1}{4}$ by $1\frac{1}{2}$ ins.   O By both sexes, mainly by female. 24-27 days. Single-brooded.

STONE-CURLEW *Burhinus œdicnemus œdicnemus* (*Linnæus*, 1758)

A c. 16 ins.   B Yellow with black tip. c. $1\frac{1}{2}$ ins.   C Dull yellow.

D Fairly large plover-like bird of open downland or heath, with streaked brown plumage, large amber-coloured eyes, and stealthy, slinking withdrawal when approached. Flight pattern of black and white on wings—two conspicuous whitish bars on basal part. Flight direct with regular, rather slow wing-beats. Wild wailing cries, particularly at dusk.

E Wailing " coor-lee "—hence name, Stone Curlew—often followed by wild medley of notes. Other variants during breeding.

F Ground display by both birds bending stiffly, bills touching ground, hind parts elevated. Also leapings and wing fannings. Nest-relief ceremony varied. Often presentation of small stones. Injury-feigning and " false preening " recorded.

G Mainly snails, slugs, worms and insects. Mice and young birds recorded.

H Central and southern Europe from Baltic to Mediterranean. *British Isles:* Summer resident S.E. counties (? Yorks), and some winter in S.W. England.

J European birds winter W. France, Iberian peninsula, N.W. and E. Africa and S. Arabia. *British Isles:* Summer residents arrive S. coast (Dorset eastwards) mid-March and April. Flock mid-August to September, sometimes 50 or more. Most leave by end of October.

K Open country—barren stony plains and semi-desert country.

L In Britain—chalk uplands, sandy heaths: occasionally sand dunes and extensive pebble beaches. In Norfolk—bare heaths amongst pine plantations.

M Scrape on bare flint-strewn ground. Small stones and rabbit droppings often added.

N Normally 2. Yellowish-stone irregularly streaked and blotched with sepia. c. $2\frac{1}{10}$ by $1\frac{1}{2}$ ins.

O By both sexes. 25-27 days. Normally single-brooded.

Distribution Maps of Waders breeding regularly in the British Isles
(after W. B. Alexander and James Fisher)

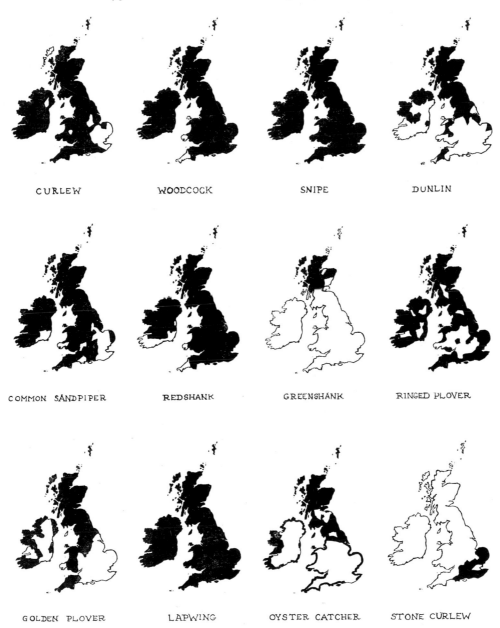

CURLEW   WOODCOCK   SNIPE   DUNLIN

COMMON SANDPIPER   REDSHANK   GREENSHANK   RINGED PLOVER

GOLDEN PLOVER   LAPWING   OYSTER CATCHER   STONE CURLEW

These maps have been prepared by shading in those areas (*vice* counties) from which breeding records have been reported. Though giving a comprehensive survey of the extent of breeding, they do not convey any idea of its density. For example, there are possibly only two pairs of Curlews nesting each year in the whole of Sussex. A similar area in Scotland might well have several thousand nesting birds. Again, the tendency for isolated pairs of Ringed Plovers to nest far inland makes the breeding-distribution map of this bird appear to be untrue to its known character as a coastal species.

*Breeding records in the present century of Waders that nest sparsely
or sporadically in the British Isles*

1. *Black-Tailed Godwit*   Lincolnshire (1 pair), 1940, 1941.
    Caithness (1 pair), 1946.

2. *Whimbrel*   Sparsely distributed in Orkneys, Shetlands, N. Sutherland, Inverness (since 1931), O. Hebrides.

3. *Red-Necked Phalarope*   Orkneys, Shetlands, O. Hebrides, I. Hebrides (Tiree), Co. Mayo. Sparsely localised.

4. *Temminck's Stint*   Cairngorms, 1934, 1936. (1 pair. Eggs laid, but unsuccessful.)

5. *Ruff*   Durham, 1901-4. Yorks, 1902. Norfolk, 1907, 1922. Lancs, 1910.

6. *Green Sandpiper*   Westmorland, 1917. (Running young found.)

7. *Northern Golden Plover*   St. Kilda, 1948. (1 pair.)

8. *Little Ringed Plover*   Herts, 1938 *et seq.* Middlesex, 1944 *et seq.* 11 pairs at least in " London area " in 1947. Suffolk and Yorks, 1948. Sussex, 1949.

9. *Kentish Plover*   Kent-Sussex coast: regularly to 1931, sporadically since.

10. *Dotterel*   Sparsely localised in Westmorland and Cumberland, Cairngorms, Grampians, E. Ross, Kircudbright, Angus, Roxburgh, W. Ross, Dumfries.

11. *Black-Winged Stilt*   Nottingham, 1945. (3 nests.)

12. *Avocet*   Ireland, 1938. (2 pairs. Locality not disclosed.) Suffolk, 1947 (at least 7 nests), 1948. 1949.

See map opposite

162